The media's watching Vault! Here's a sampling of our coverage.

"Lawyers looking for the scoop on the nation's biggest law firms now have a place to go."
– ***The Wall Street Journal***

"With reviews and profiles of firms that one associate calls 'spot on', [Vault's] guide has become a key reference for those who want to know what it takes to get hired by a law firm and what to expect once they get there."
– ***New York Law Journal***

"The best place on the web to prepare for a job search."
– ***Fortune***

"Vault is indispensable for locating insider information."
– ***Metropolitan Corporate Counsel***

"[Vault's guide] is an INVALUABLE Cliff's Notes to prepare for interviews."
– ***Women's Lawyer's Journal***

"For those hoping to climb the ladder of success, [Vault's] insights are priceless."
– ***Money Magazine***

"[Vault guides] make for excellent starting points for job hunters and should be purchased by academic libraries for their career sections [and] university career centers."
– ***Library Journal***

VAULT
> the most trusted name in career information™

Explorers know.
It's called teaming.
We're a law firm with an uncommon practice—organizing our practice around clients. Not your typical service team of deal or IP lawyers, but a multidisciplinary group drawn together to focus on the client's environment, their goals and their challenges. No matter how daunting.
To learn more about doing high performance work as part of a high performing team, visit us at www.pillsburywinthrop.com.
Teams that work.
PILLSBURY WINTHROP LLP
www.pillsburywinthrop.com

VAULT GUIDE TO
CORPORATE LAW CAREERS

VAULT GUIDE TO CORPORATE LAW CAREERS

ZAHIE EL KOURI
AND THE STAFF OF VAULT

Library of Congress Cataloging-in-Publication Data

El Kouri, Zahie.
Vault guide to corporate law careers / Zahie El Kouri and the staff of Vault.
p. cm.
ISBN 1-58131-222-9
1. Corporate lawyers--United States. 2. Law--Vocational guidance--United States. I. Title: Corporate law careers. II. Vault (Firm) III. Title.
KF299.I5E416 2003
346.73'066'023--dc21

2003011388

Printed in the United States of America

ACKNOWLEDGEMENTS

From Zahie El Kouri: I would like to acknowledge the extraordinary assistance and support of Katharine Hartland, Jennifer Yates, Stephanie Waidner, Ann Winfield, John MacEachern, Leigh Scales, Simone Singletary, Stacey Lewis, Sara Staben, Kathryn Kollett, John Greenman, Catherine Curan, Caroline Berger, Vivian Hood, Robert Brown, Anna Rabinowitz and Naim and Silva El Kouri.

Special thanks to Marcy Lerner, Vera Djordjevich, and the many attorneys and career services advisors who gave generously of their time and expertise.

From Vault: Vault like to thank Matt Doull, Ahmad Al-Khaled, Lee Black, Eric Ober, Hollinger Ventures, Tekbanc, New York City Investment Fund, Globix, Hoover's, Glenn Fischer, Mark Hernandez, Ravi Mhatre, Carter Weiss, Ken Cron, Ed Somekh, Isidore Mayrock, Zahi Khouri, Sana Sabbagh, and other Vault investors, as well as our family and friends.

Table of Contents

Wildman Harrold
Attorneys and Counselors

The results are in . . .

Our mid-level associates ranked us:

- 3rd best overall firm in Chicago
- 9th best large firm nationally
- 1st in Management Openness among Chicago firms
- 1st in Communications Regarding Partnership among Chicago firms
- 5th best nationwide in Partner-Associate Relations

American Lawyer Mid-Level Associate Survey, 2002

Wildman Harrold's corporate lawyers provide clients with a full-range of transactional and corporate counseling services to publicly and privately held domestic and international businesses, including in acquisition and divestitures, M&A's, asset sales, leveraged buyouts, private equity investments, loan financings, executive compensation arrangements and strategic alliances.

Our corporate lawyers work with clients in forming and structuring domestic and international joint ventures, partnerships, limited liability companies and corporations. They also handle registered public offerings and private placements of securities. The firm acts regularly as issuers' counsel for a number of entities and has a thriving SBIC/Venture Capital practice and a strong Tax group. Check us out at www.wildmanharrold.com.

Contact: Sue Cicero
Recruiting Coordinator
cicero@wildmanharrold.com

225 West Wacker Drive
Chicago, Illinois 60606
312.201.2000

2300 Cabot Drive
Lisle, Illinois 60532
630.955.0555

Clements Inn
London, England
WC2A 2AZ
011.44.20.7831.0009

www.wildmanharrold.com

global vision
New York
Palo Alto
Paris
Washington, D.C.
Manchester
Los Angeles
London
Houston
Frankfurt
Cologne
Chicago
Charlotte
Brussels
As one of the worlds 10 largest law firms, we offer attorneys great opportunities to expand their horizons. And yet, each of our 13 offices is distinguished by a culture that emphasizes close ties to and understanding of the surrounding community.
For the name of a recruitment contact in any of our offices, visit our career opportunities web site at www.mayerbrownrowe.com/careeropportunities.
local focus
MAYER
BROWN
ROWE
& MAW

Introduction

CHAPTER 1

If litigators go to court, what exactly do corporate lawyers do? Television might have left you only with the vague impression that corporate lawyers work in big offices, wear nice suits, meet with high-powered clients and get paid a lot of money. It's true that corporate law can be a prestigious, well-paid and challenging career, but, as any practicing attorney will tell you, there's a lot more to working life than fancy offices, headline-making clients and hefty paychecks. Before you decide whether to join their ranks, you should have a more realistic sense of what corporate lawyers really do.

Take Kaplan.
Score higher.
178
on the LSAT*
out of a possible 180
(99th percentile)
"Kaplan gave me the confidence I needed to ace the test and get into Harvard Law."
Alexandria Marzano-Lesnevich
Edison, NJ
Kaplan LSAT student
World Leader in Test Prep
KAPLAN
1-800-KAP-TEST
kaptest.com
*Test names are registered trademarks of their respective owners. The scores of individual students will vary. The experience of these students cannot be taken as an indicator of how the average student or students in general will perform.

THE SCOOP

Corporate Law Basics

CHAPTER 2

What is Corporate Law?

Corporate law is the law of corporations. A corporation is an artificial legal entity, typically chartered by a state and formed in order to operate a business. Once chartered, the corporation is completely separate from its owners, is liable for its own debts and must pay its own taxes.

But many lawyers deal with corporations, and not all of them call themselves corporate lawyers. In fact, at this point, you might not have a clear idea of the differences among a litigator who works in-house for a corporation, a tax lawyer who advises corporations from the vantage point of a law firm and a corporate lawyer. If you watch too much television, you might believe that lawyers represent clients on deals one day and head to the courtroom for high-profile litigation the next. This is highly unusual in the real practice of law. While both litigators and corporate lawyers deal with corporations, they do so in very different ways.

Litigation versus transactional law

One of the basic divisions in the practice of law is between litigation and corporate, or transactional, law. Litigation attorneys, or litigators, deal with the judicial process, with civil disputes or criminal cases that are headed to court. In the realm of criminal law, they are prosecutors, public defenders or private defense attorneys. Those attorneys who handle conflicts between individuals, whether over personal injuries, domestic disputes or other matters, are civil trial lawyers. Commercial litigators are trial attorneys whose clients include corporations and businesses.

Note that being a litigator doesn't automatically put you in a courtroom. Public defenders may indeed be in court every week. But litigators who work on corporate or commercial matters might never go to court. They serve their clients by filing motions and briefs and settling conflicts without actually going to trial.

It's a myth that everyone who wants to be a lawyer wants to spend time in a courtroom. Many people don't have any interest in criminal law or personal injury. Some would rather contribute to the creation of a business venture than participate in its breakdown. Some lawyers don't care to write the (many) documents that must be submitted to court. Attorneys who facilitate transactions in the fields of corporate or tax law, intellectual property or employee benefits are considered transactional lawyers. In the world of business, transactional lawyers try to set up deals in a way that will avoid litigation and make clear the rights and responsibilities of all parties in the event that something does go wrong.

The difference between corporate law and commercial litigation is simple. Corporate lawyers build transactions or deals, and litigators deal with transactions gone wrong, whether through the judicial system or through alternative methods of dispute resolution like mediation or arbitration.

Transactional law and corporate lawyers

So, what is a corporate lawyer? Basically, corporate lawyers advise businesses on their legal obligations, rights and responsibilities. People who call themselves corporate lawyers are usually corporate generalists, lawyers who provide advice on how to structure a business and evaluate ventures and who coordinate with specialists, like tax lawyers, employee benefits lawyers and real estate attorneys (who are all transactional lawyers), to serve the sophisticated needs of their corporate clients.

While corporate attorneys may provide day-to-day advice to their clients, most of their work, at least in larger law firms, is transactional in nature. In fact, some firms use the terms "transactional" and "corporate" interchangeably when describing areas of practice. Corporate lawyers structure transactions, draft documents, review other lawyers' agreements, negotiate deals, attend meetings and make calls toward those ends. A corporate lawyer ensures that the provisions of an agreement are clear, unambiguous and won't cause problems for their client in the future. Corporate attorneys also advise on the duties and responsibilities of corporate officers, directors and insiders.

There are many varieties of corporate law practice, and not all corporate lawyers do the same kind of work. Moreover, not all firms categorize corporate practice in the same way. For example, some firms might have separate practice groups for antitrust or mergers & acquisitions, while others include them within their corporate department. The following list, while not exhaustive, outlines some of the areas in which corporate attorneys might spend their time.

Areas of Corporate Practice

Corporate formation, governance and operation

A corporation is a legal entity created through the laws of its state of incorporation. Individual states make laws relating to the creation, organization and dissolution of corporations. The law treats a corporation as a legal "person" that has the standing to sue and be sued, and is distinct from its stockholders. The legal independence of a corporation prevents shareholders from being personally liable for corporate debts. The legal person status of corporations gives the business perpetual life; the death (or, in today's climate, discrediting) of an official or a major stockholder does not alter the corporation's structure, even if it affects the stock price.

A corporate lawyer can help a client create, organize or dissolve a business entity. To form a corporation, an attorney drafts articles of incorporation, which document the creation of the company and specify the management of internal affairs. Most states require a corporation to have bylaws defining the roles of officers of the company. Corporate lawyers also deal with business entities in the forms of partnerships, limited liability companies, limited liability partnerships and business trusts; each form has its own set of legal rights and responsibilities, organizational structure and tax burdens. Attorneys help their clients decide which of these legal forms is best suited for the business they want to run and the relationships the principals want to build with each other.

A corporate lawyer who helps a client form a company might later be called upon for other legal advice related to the start-up or management of the business, like reviewing a lease for office space or equipment, or drafting employment contracts, non-disclosure and non-compete agreements. Corporate lawyers might research aspects of employment law or environmental law or consult with another attorney who specializes in that field. Business executives also seek advice from corporate attorneys on the rights and responsibilities of corporate directors and officers.

Mergers & acquisitions

One major corporate practice area is mergers and acquisitions ("M&A"). Through acquiring (buying) or merging with another company, a business might add property, production facilities or a brand name. A merger or acquisition might also work to neutralize a competitor in the same field. Corporate attorneys provide legal counsel about proposed transactions. To help evaluate a proposed venture, a corporate lawyer (who typically relies on a team of corporate lawyers) reviews all of the company's key assets and liabilities, meaning financial statements, employment agreements, real estate holdings, intellectual property holdings and any current, pending or likely litigation. This is called due diligence. The corporate lawyer can then assess the situation and raise specific issues with the client – for example, who's responsible for the Environmental Protection Agency investigation of that piece of property the company owns? What happens to the employees of the target company or to the stock options of the company's directors?

Corporate lawyers consult with their clients about these questions and together lawyer and client determine which parties should accept current or potential liabilities. The lawyers then draft the merger or acquisition agreement and negotiate in detail the terms of each party's rights, responsibilities and liabilities.

Venture capital

In a venture capital practice, a lawyer works on private and public financings and day-to-day counseling. This means they help new businesses find money for their ventures, organize their operations and maintain their legal and business structures after formation. In venture capital, as in any corporate law position dealing with emerging companies, lawyers help build and expand businesses. Their responsibilities can include general corporate work, like drafting articles of incorporation and other documents, as well as technology licensing, financing, and mergers & acquisitions.

Some lawyers find this type of work less confrontational than M&A practice because the client is working with other parties toward a common goal. Sometimes, in mergers & acquisitions, the parties see the process as a zero-sum game in which each must get the best deal no matter how it may affect future relations with the other company. This is especially the case in hostile acquisitions.

Project finance

The development and construction of power plants, oil refineries, industrial plants, pipelines, mines, telecommunications networks and facilities and transportation systems involve the cooperation of many different entities, many different lawyers and extremely large sums of money. Project finance attorneys specialize in these deals. They form a project entity, a corporation, partnership or other legal entity that will exist for the term of the project, and they draft power purchase agreements and construction contracts and negotiate financial terms with lenders and investors

Corporate securities

Some corporate lawyers specialize in corporate securities law. On a federal level, the Securities Act of 1933 requires companies who sell securities to the public to register with the federal government. Corporations must follow certain protocols regarding disclosure of information to shareholders and investors depending on the size of the corporation and the type of investor. If shares of a company's stock are traded on a public stock exchange, the company has to file detailed reports with the Securities and Exchange Commission and distribute parts of those reports (the prospectus) to shareholders. The Securities Act of 1934 addresses the obligations of companies traded on a national stock exchange.

To ensure the companies remain in accordance with these laws, corporate attorneys prepare reports for initial public offerings, yearly and quarterly disclosures, and special disclosures whenever something happens that might affect the price of the stock, like impending litigation, government investigation or disappointing financial results. Even if you don't specialize in corporate securities law, the issuance of stock and the creation and distribution of the reports are subject to a whole host of rules with which corporate lawyers must be familiar.

Intellectual property

Corporate lawyers often advise their clients on intellectual property matters. Intellectual property law can include research and analysis of trade secret issues, patent and trademark licensing and protection, software licensing and copyright law.

Non-legal roles

Business clients frequently look to their lawyers for advice directly related to the operation of their business but only tangentially related to the law, such as how to deal with special interest groups, how to respond to concerns about product safety, whether to fire an executive, how to plan for the possibility of adverse media coverage, how to create a business plan, how to cope with a serious ethical lapse, whether to close a factory and what kind of compensation plans should be offered to employees.

Related Practice Areas

Other lawyers may deal with the same types of clients and the same transactions as corporate lawyers, but they have more specialized fields of expertise.

Tax law

Corporations are taxable entities subject to their own tax laws from individuals. Although corporations have a "double tax" problem – both corporate profits and shareholder dividends are taxed – corporate profits are taxed at a lower rate than rates for individuals. The practice of corporate tax lawyers covers all sorts of business planning, and attorneys often give tax advice to their firm's clients in connection with an acquisition transaction. Tax lawyers must understand the business situations of clients and stay on top of developments in tax law. They research issues in the tax codes, related journals and reporters, and keep in touch with Internal Revenue Service attorneys.

Real estate law

Real estate lawyers can help corporations purchase and sell property, finance the purchases, and coordinate with environmental and litigation lawyers as necessary. A real estate attorney structures real estate transactions and drafts purchase agreements. He or she might deal with construction contracts, property management agreements, zoning and land use issues. If you're practicing real estate law in a big firm, your client will likely be a corporation, and you'll have to deal with financing as sophisticated as that handled by a regular corporate lawyer.

Banking and finance law

Banking lawyers advise clients in the financial services industry. They represent borrowers, lenders and other participants in agreements to finance business ventures. In addition to working on transaction documents, these lawyers have to deal with various regulations of financial institutions monitored by the Federal Reserve Board and other government agencies.

Bankruptcy law

Bankruptcy lawyers represent debtors and creditors in resolutions of their monetary obligations under the U.S. Bankruptcy Code. The Code is intended to help organizations and individuals come up with a plan to pay off debts and reorder their financial affairs. Chapter 7 of the Bankruptcy Code deals with liquidation and Chapter 11, a much more common way to resolve business debt, covers business reorganization. With the downturn of the economy, the downsizing of companies and the increase in bankruptcy filings, many corporate lawyers these days are involved in restructuring.

Employee benefits

Employee benefits lawyers advise clients on executive compensation programs and employee benefit plans. They help corporations design, implement and terminate compensation and benefit plans, and they review and modify employee benefit plans in mergers and acquisitions. Employee benefits plans can include pension, profit-sharing, employee stock ownership and 401(k) plans. In addition to drafting and negotiating these agreements, employee benefits attorneys also research the implications of tax laws and the Employment Retirement Income Security Act (ERISA).

As you can see, all these transactional lawyers structure different kinds of deals or transactions or parts of deals or transactions. Much of what this book will say about the life and work of a corporate lawyer will also apply to the life and work of other transactional attorneys.

The Corporate Lawyer

CHAPTER 3

The Law Firm

Now that you've been introduced to different varieties of corporate law practice, you might be trying to picture your life as an attorney. So the next thing you need to know is where this work takes place.

Most corporate lawyers practice in medium-sized to large law firms at some point in their careers. After a period of training at such a firm, many attorneys either become employed directly by corporations or move to smaller firms. Some corporate lawyers work for government agencies at the federal, state or local level, white others set up their own solo practices or even launch their own businesses.

A law firm is a group of lawyers who practice together as a formal entity. In the past, law firms were all organized as general partnerships, but now they may be professional corporations, limited liability partnerships or limited liability companies. Law firms can consist of two lawyers or several hundred lawyers. Attorneys who take a share of firm profits are called partners, principals or shareholders. Lawyers who work for a salary are associates.

A third category of lawyers includes "of counsel" or "special counsel." These attorneys are more senior than associates but not partners. They work out their own payment structure with the firm, in some cases receiving a share of the profits from clients they bring in or service, but not a share of what the other lawyers in the firm bring in, and in other cases receiving payment as salaried employees.

In addition to the attorneys, whether partner, associate or of counsel, many law firms also employ paralegals and legal assistants. Paralegals often do much of the same work as junior associates, but without a law degree (and for much less money). Attorneys are responsible for the work a paralegal does, but a paralegal with a great deal of experience will often know more about his or her field than the lawyers. Some paralegals work on general research and filings, while others might specialize in real estate closings or corporate securities filings. Not all firms have paralegals, but for most large firms paralegals can be a very cost-effective solution to lower-level tasks. Most associates also have some access to a secretary or legal assistant, although they will rarely have that person's undivided attention. A secretary or legal assistant can screen your calls, type handwritten corrections on documents and help you with other paperwork.

There are other people who make a law firm work. Many firms have a dedicated word processing staff, often divided into a day shift and a night shift. These people can be an invaluable resource to you when you're stuck all night in the office with a partner, a deadline and a huge stack of documents to revise. Some firms have a business development or marketing department responsible for producing the marketing materials partners use to get clients. This staff might also be responsible for maintaining the firm's web site and tracking and distributing news about recent deals and trials. And then there are the people who run the business end of the law firm: the accounting department, the payroll department and the office manager, all of whom are very important to an associate's well-being.

The Legal Job Market

Maybe you know you want to be a corporate lawyer, but wonder whether corporate law is a smart career move in the current economy. In a time of accounting shenanigans, corporate scandals and personal bankruptcies, people commonly joke that the lawyers are the only ones making money. Many students opt for law school or business school instead of immediate entry into the corporate world. But, lawyer jokes aside, the truth is that the job market for attorneys is much slower than it was 10 years ago.

But before you even worry about landing a job, you have to get into law school. The past few years have brought a dramatic increase in the number of students applying to law school. Georgetown University received 11,500 applications for the fall 2003 semester – the largest number of applications ever received by an American law school. Nationwide, applications to law schools accredited by the American Bar Association have risen by 18.5 percent. In a weak economy, it's harder to find jobs of any kind, and talented and ambitious students see law school as an opportunity to wait out the hard times and emerge a more competitive candidate when more jobs are likely to be available. But when everyone is thinking the same thing, admission becomes a much tougher game.

And once you're in law school, the competition doesn't get any easier. The current legal job market began a decline in mid-2001. Gone are the days of law firm summer clerkships full of perks, easy hours and tons of money. Gone, too, are the days of a guaranteed offer from your summer position. Legal jobs are now more difficult to get and easier to lose. A survey of law firms by the National Association for Law Placement (NALP) shows that the economic downturn has caused over 22 percent of legal employers to implement associate hiring freezes. Over 18 percent of the employers actually laid off associates, even at top firms. Even associates who weren't restricted from obtaining or keeping jobs, were likely affected by the market's decline. Forty-nine percent of NALP member law firms cut the budgets of their recruiting department, and 35 percent stopped hiring new support staff.

There is, however, some good news – the market may have hit bottom. Law school placement officers believe that hiring in 2003 won't be worse than it was in 2002, and it may actually be a bit better. Firms cut back on hiring so much last year that they don't need to cut much more.

As you make your career decisions, there are two things to keep in mind: first, there will always be good jobs for good lawyers, and second, markets are cyclical. Attorneys have faced tough job markets before, and they have survived them. The work you put in now, at the beginning of your corporate job search, will make a difference for your future success, whether you're a practicing attorney in a different field, a first-year associate or a law student.

Is Corporate Law Right for You?

One associate explains his decision to go to law school: "I picked law because the option of going to law school is the simplest sort of big-picture planning around. That is, you sign up, then follow the rules and a path is laid out for you to follow. As long as you can work hard and more or less intelligently, signing up for law school resolves the 'what the hell do I do now?' question pretty well."

This associate is not alone in his motivation. If you're looking for a career that will give you status, money and a chance to use your brain for sophisticated work in the private sector, law could be your answer. But is corporate law the answer? How can you know whether corporate law is the right direction for your career? There are other kinds of law that will give you the same advantages. How can you know if corporate law is right for you?

Corporate practice versus commercial litigation

Commercial litigators can practice in the same kinds of law firms, work for the same kinds of clients and make the same kind of money as corporate lawyers. So how do prospective lawyers know what type of law will suit them?

Some people are attracted to the idea of advocacy, but feel that they can accomplish more with a field of law that focuses on building structures rather than challenging them. At its best, corporate law finances small companies, helps them grow and provide jobs for people. Some corporate lawyers find litigation reactive and adversarial rather than constructive and preemptive. Furthermore, corporate deals enjoy a wider turn around and shorter time frames for completing projects, while litigation can drag on for years. On the other hand, according to one associate, "If you want to practice corporate because you think litigation is confrontational, you might want to examine your suitability for the practice of law in general. Any type of law can be contentious and stressful if you're at a big firm or have an important corporate client."

Francesca Lavin, a senior associate at Cleary, Gottlieb, Steen & Hamilton in New York, suggests that law students "try to find summer jobs where they can try out both litigation and corporate work." Many students end up in litigation because they have more exposure to it in law school or because they have strong verbal skills, when in fact they might be happier in the corporate arena. Lavin believes that communication skills are "just as important in the transactional setting as they are in litigation." The most effective corporate lawyers are those who can communicate persuasively and think quickly on their feet.

Narrowing the field

Once you get past the litigation-versus-transaction decision, there are fewer easy answers. There is no one set of attributes that separates a successful and satisfied real estate lawyer from a successful and satisfied corporate lawyer. All good lawyers must be able to communicate with their clients in an effective manner. This means that they have to be able both to listen and to explain legal circumstances in a clear, precise and personable fashion. Because corporate attorneys often have to consult with accountants, bankers and various employees of the companies they represent, they also have to be able to communicate well with non-lawyers.

Corporate lawyers should enjoy and be good at problem-solving. They must be able to analyze the difficulties of a situation and make choices about what to do to make things best for their client. Corporate attorneys must be comfortable with numbers. Corporate law is about business, and business is about money. One junior associate says that students considering corporate law should know that "you will sit at a desk and be a paper-pusher, probably all your life." You may be on the phone for much of the day and do a lot of negotiating, but you will do it most often sitting at your desk or huddled in a conference room.

Of course, all these attributes are required of other transactional attorneys as well. The truth is that, while you might be able to tell whether you want to do litigation before you try it, you may not be able to discover the area of transactional law you love until you are exposed to it, either in a class or on the job.

If, for example, you have a real facility with numbers, you might want to consider tax law. In fact, even if you don't consider it, and you show an aptitude, your firm may simply direct you to that area. Not everyone enjoys working with numbers or has such a proficiency, and those that do can find an excellent niche in tax law while still participating in the deal-making aspects of corporate law.

John DeRosa, assistant dean of career services at Cornell, offers advice to the prospective corporate lawyer: "Try early on, ideally before law school, to learn as much as you possibly can about the practice of law, and the practice of corporate law, both to learn what it is you might be spending your work life doing and to learn what to do to be competitive as a law school candidate, and as an associate. If you put in a little effort as a first year, like going to hear alums, talking to faculty, it will be very easy to get information. In fact," DeRosa cautions that informational interviews "will be easier before law school and during your first year. Since you're not actually trying to get a job through the meeting, the lawyers you talk to will be a lot more comfortable because they'll be able to tell that you don't want anything other than information. If you can go into your second year of law school having spoken to a few corporate lawyers and some faculty members, you'll be in good shape. You'll not only know whether or not this is for you, you'll have a better sense of what to say in an interview."

GETTING HIRED

Getting Hired: Law School

CHAPTER 4

The Credentials

What does it take to get hired as a corporate lawyer? For starters, you have to have the right credentials. Law firms will look at the schools you attend and the other firms for which you've worked. If and when you see clients, they're going to look up your profile on your firm's web site or in the Martindale-Hubbell Law Directory; at the very least, they'll take a look at the diplomas hanging on the walls of your office.

Before Law School

Undergraduate education

While it might seem that the first credential you need to become a corporate lawyer is law school, your undergraduate degree can also be very important. The most obvious reason is that your undergraduate record and the caliber of the institution from which you earn it can determine where you go to law school. A less obvious advantage is the alumni network you gain from your college. Some people are much more loyal to their undergraduate alma mater than to any other affiliation they share with a prospective job candidate. This can help you connect with a potential employer on an interview, even help you get an interview in the first place. There are two ways to maximize the credential value of your undergraduate education: either go to a nationally ranked school and come out with solid (or better) grades or go to a lower-ranked school and come out with stellar grades.

While most law schools don't require any specific classes as a prerequisite to admission, some undergraduate courses can make the experience of law school and the practice of corporate law easier.

- **Substantive knowledge.** Some lawyers recommend that you take classes dealing with subjects that might come up in your life as a lawyer. Classes on business, accounting and economics can expose you to financial and business concepts and help you figure out which area of transactional or corporate law you're interested in. And even if you still don't know what kind of law you want to practice, these classes can give you a head start on some of the information you'll need to know for your practice.

- **Broader intellectual development.** Others suggest thinking of your broader intellectual development. Because law schools don't require any particular courses, prospective law school candidates can choose classes they're interested in. Since most lawyers will have little time for intellectual or artistic pursuits once they start practicing, college can be a great time to learn about anthropology or history or to take a class in drawing or sculpture.

- **Reading and writing critically.** The third approach is to develop your capacity for reading and writing analytically. These are skills that will be indispensable to the analysis and distillation of case law each law student has to do on a daily basis. And the ability to assimilate, assess and modify information will be crucial to your success as a lawyer.

When asked what a student might do to prepare for a career as a corporate attorney, the response of one junior associate at a large firm was both immediate and emphatic: "Take accounting, take accounting, take accounting." There is no one right answer to the question of what other classes an aspiring corporate lawyer should take as an undergraduate. The lawyers who recommend you take business and pre-law classes have the same sorts of jobs to those who recommend you take sculpture and history. Certainly, many successful lawyers enter law school with little to no prior study of business, finance or law. If you do think you want to pursue corporate law, however, it might be a good idea to figure out how interested you are in the world of business and corporations, since the majority of your waking life will be spent thinking about them.

Work experience

For many years, business schools have required a certain number of years of work experience before admission. While law schools haven't adopted the same strategy, it is undeniable that such experience can prove very useful, and more and more law students are coming in with prior work experience. For example, Steve McCormick, a Kirkland & Ellis recruiting partner, cites his alma mater Northwestern University Law School, where two-thirds of the 2002-2003 first-year law students have at least one year of work experience and one-third have three years or more. "This work experience isn't necessarily law-related," explains McCormick. "The biggest advantage comes from experiential maturity, the perspective of living an adult life, of getting up and going to work every day."

Sam Kim, a mid-level Boston associate at Lucash, Gesmer & Updegrove, agrees. "I was a commissioned officer in the United States Navy for four years. I recommend that everyone go and work or do something other than going straight to law school after college. You need time away from the academic world to discover yourself a little bit – for example, finding out what you're good at and what you find passion in, in order to examine whether you really want to practice law. The question should not be whether you want to go to law school. The question should be whether you want to be in the legal profession. It is too expensive an investment, money- and time-wise, to jump into law school right after college. The work experience also gives you a better perspective in law school because you already go in with confidence in who you are and what you are capable of, instead of hanging your self-worth/value purely on your performance in law school."

This doesn't mean that you need work experience to get into law school, or even to land your first summer job during law school. "Work experience in an investment bank or other corporate environment can be helpful, but not necessary or important," says John DeRosa. "Large firms are very selective in certain ways: they tend to look very closely at grades, the kind of school you're coming out of, and so on, but in terms of background the large firms are open-minded. They're looking for interesting, refined backgrounds, which can be in performing arts or public service in addition to experience in the corporate world. In a large firm you're brought along so slowly and you're trained so much along the way that experience is not necessary. Work experience as a paralegal can give a more informed sense of what this profession offers, and maybe even a stronger legal skill set. But so many other factors come into play that experience as a paralegal won't dramatically improve your chances of getting hired."

"A corporate background would help to warn a person ahead of time what it's like inside the walls of corporate America – sitting in an office and dealing with the suited (or now business casual) masses," says one associate. According to another lawyer, "The attorneys who seem to have the most advantage from prior careers (besides the general experience gained in any job) are those who work with securities and previously worked as CPAs or analysts at investment banks or those who practice tax law and have a background in accounting."

Even if you don't work in a law firm or corporation, try to find out as much as you can about practicing law before you go to law school. It can help you decide whether to be a lawyer, choose whether to be a corporate lawyer and give more focus to your law school experience. One great way to do this is to schedule informational interviews with practicing attorneys in as many areas of law as you can and ask them lots of questions.

Choosing a Law School

Law school is a prerequisite for practicing corporate law. (There are a few states, like Vermont, in which you can become a lawyer by working as a paralegal for a number of years before taking the bar exam, but this is an unusual phenomenon, and taking a path does not usually lead to jobs in corporate law.) Many lawyers agree that law school does not prepare you to be a lawyer. Even more agree that law school does not prepare you to be a transactional lawyer. The law student mantra is that law school teaches you to "think like a lawyer." Lawyers disagree on whether this is myth or fact. What is true is that graduating from a reputable law school can give you the opportunity to find a challenging, high-paying entry-level job. This is an opportunity few people have. In the long run, the law school experience is a necessary evil. Survive it, excel at it and it will serve you well.

In a weak economy, both students fresh out of college and people with significant work experience look to graduate and professional schools as a refuge from the job market. Law school applications were up almost 18 percent for the 2002-2003 school year, the biggest spike in two decades. This means 88,418 applications nationwide. At some schools the increase in applications and the number of students accepting offers of admission was so great that it threw off the formula that lets law schools plan for the number of students in an entering class. It's rumored that at one school the entering class for 2002-2003 was three times as large as those for previous years, forcing the law school to hire several more faculty members to teach sections of first-year courses. The same has not been true of medical schools and business schools, probably because each of these require more years of preparation and planning (medical school requires premed courses, while applicants for business school must have work experience.)

Other than bar admissions, the law school you attend is likely the most important credential you can add to your resume. There are many factors to consider in choosing a law school. The top three are reputation, money and location.

Reputation

Reputation is a subjective quality, usually based on other subjective qualities and usually measured in national rankings and local prestige.

Every year, the magazine *U.S. News & World Report* publishes an issue devoted to ranking the colleges and universities of the United States. This is the ranking that people talk about for law schools. The magazine looks at subjective factors like ratings by academics, lawyers and judges, as well as statistical data like LSAT (Law School Aptitude Test) scores, bar passage rates, and acceptance and rejection rates. It conducts opinion polls and gathers statistics on average LSAT scores and undergraduate grade point averages (GPAs). Employers often use the rankings to determine which schools merit an on-campus interviewing visit. And, in a chicken and egg way, the fact that the law firms are paying more attention to those law schools leads to better applicants at those schools, since that's where law students see good career prospects. If you've missed the latest print issue, you can review the rankings online at http://www.usnews.com..

National ranking systems like those published by *U.S. News* have been criticized for subjectivity and an overdependence on reputation without consideration of issues like who gets jobs, what graduates think of their law school, and so on. Some critics, including a coalition of law school deans, have come up with alternative rankings. For more information about alternative rankings and criticism of subjective national rankings, refer to "Judging the Law Schools," an "unauthorized ranking" of law schools by Thomas E. Brennan, a former Chief Justice of the Michigan Supreme Court (www.ilrg.com/rankings/), and "The Ranking Game," from Indiana University School of Law-Bloomington (http://monoborg.law.indiana.edu/LawRank/index.html). However, most lawyers and clients still use the *US News* rankings as a yardstick of prestige

A school that ranks in the top of the *U.S. News* list, a "national" law school, offers advantages in the form of portability of degree. Students who attend national schools typically have an easier time finding jobs in different geographical regions than do those coming from lower-ranked schools. A national school may also have highly regarded faculty. "I went to the best law school I got into and would encourage everyone to do the same," says a Harvard alum working in a large Boston firm. "Law school is about getting a credential and access to the career, not an experience onto itself. It's called a professional school for a reason."

Of course, many successful corporate lawyers haven't gone to Harvard or Yale. A local school can be an excellent strategic and financially sound decision, especially for someone who knows the geographic area in which he wants to practice. And all firms hire from the top of their local school class. "I have realized that if you don't get into a top-10 national school, it is sometimes better to go to a local school with many local connections to firms than to go to a second-tier national school in a state in which you won't practice," says a Boston associate. "For example, people in Boston who went to Boston College Law School have good luck landing jobs in firms even though there are a lot of second-tier national schools ranked above them."

If you're lucky enough to get into several schools with good programs in areas of law which interest you, then you just need to think about personal comfort. This is where money and location come into play.

Other law school and law placement resources:

- National Association for Law Placement: http://www.nalp.org/
- Law School Admission Council: www.lsac.org
- The Boston College Law School Locator: http://www.bc.edu/bc_org/svp/carct/matrix.html.

The law locator matrix, which lists the 25th to 75th percentile LSAT scores and GPA ranges of first-year classes at accredited law schools, can help you determine safety schools, schools for which you are competitive and "reaches."

Money

Law school is an investment, and you need to think about how much you are willing and able to invest for the returns you might get from this credential. An associate in Minneapolis offers this perspective: "The choice an applicant faces may be between going to a more highly ranked and perhaps more expensive school versus a local school a few ranks down but which may be cheaper or may offer scholarship money. When it comes to hiring, local firms will know the local schools, and even the leading firms who typically search nationally for new associates will be willing to take a look at the better students and distinguish them from the pack. Of course," the associate adds, "you'd want to think twice before turning down a top-notch school for a mediocre one, but when the difference in prestige among your options is not great, the local choice may often make sense." And remember that superior grades will make you attractive no matter what school you attend, as will law review.

How much does it cost?

The median law school tuition is nearly $23,000 a year, and yes, this means that some people at private schools pay substantially more than that, while others at certain state schools might pay less than half. Almost all law students (94 percent) borrow money for school. On average a law student takes on $84,000 in debt.

Top Law School Tuition

RANK*	INSTITUTION	TUITION
1	Yale University	$31,400
2	Stanford University	$30,880
3	Harvard University	$29,500
4	Columbia University	$32,700
5	New York University	$32,450
6	University of Chicago	$30,714
7 (tie)	University of California – Berkeley	$22,158 (N) / $11,027 (R)
7 (tie)	University of Michigan – Ann Arbor	$30,992 (N) / $24,992 (R)
7 (tie)	University of Pennsylvania	$29,310
7 (tie)	University of Virginia	$26,967 (N) / $20,627 (R)
11	Northwestern University	$32,008
12	Duke University	$29,920
13	Cornell University	$31,250
14	Georgetown University	$29,440
15	University of Texas – Austin	$19,794(N) / $11,634(R)

R = Resident tuition, N = Non-resident tuition

**These are the U.S. News & World Report Rankings for 2002-2003 school year.*

***Estimated 2002-2003 tuition reported on law school web site.*

Top Law School Tuition cont.

RANK*	INSTITUTION	TUITION
16	University of California – Los Angeles	$22,835(N) / $11,713(R)
17	Vanderbilt University	$28,350
18 (tie)	University of Iowa	$23,668(N) / $9,910 (R)
18 (tie)	University of Minnesota	$21,604/ (N) / $12,706 (R)
18 (tie)	University of Southern California	$16,072
18 (tie)	Washington and Lee University	$10,660
22 (tie)	Boston College	$28,440
22 (tie)	Emory University	$26,318
24	University of Notre Dame	$26,400
25	Boston University	$27,222
25	George Washington University	$29,420
25	University of Illinois – Urbana-Champaign	$24,398 (N) / $11,310 (R)
25	University of Washington	$17,969(N) / $10,230(R)
25	University of Wisconsin – Madison	$24,292 (N) / $8,844 (R)
25	Washington University in St. Louis	$28,460

R = Resident tuition, N = Non-resident tuition

**These are the U.S. News & World Report Rankings for 2002-2003 school year.*

***Estimated 2002-2003 tuition reported on law school web site.*

How much can you make?

Career services offices track median starting salaries as well as law school tuitions. Associates going from a highly ranked national law school to a large law firm can start with salaries of $90,000; New York associates might start at $125,000, while associates in smaller cities or smaller firms start closer to $50,000. (Compare these figures to $39,189, the median starting salary of a public sector attorney.) It's important to factor this compensation information into your decision about how much debt to take on.

How likely is it that you'll get a job?

Law schools also track alumni employment statistics, and you should know what they are before enrolling. How many students get hired for a summer clerkship? How many have jobs when they graduate? Those statistics will tell you where the last graduating class found jobs, how many chose public interest or academia, how many are still unemployed or looking for work.

"Take a good look at the regional law school before turning down a nationally ranked alternative," advises Cornell's assistant dean of student services. "The first question you have to ask is: How extensive is the school's participation in on-campus interviewing and off-campus job fairs? But," DeRosa adds, "you can't stop there! The second question is: How deeply into the class do firms tend to hire? You might find a regional law school with 100 firms coming onto campus every year, but you have to know if they're all looking at the same small number of students. Sometimes the 100 firms interview the same 20 people. Assume you're in the middle of the class. How many interviews can you expect to get? How many offers might you expect to receive? Many law school candidates forget to ask this second question, and it's the more important question of the two."

Location

Going to law school doesn't change who you are as a person. It doesn't, with luck, change your relationships with your family and friends. It doesn't make you less apt to go to the beach instead of studying if the beach is your weakness. And it won't make you cheerful and focused during a long New England winter if you're from Southern California and prone to Seasonal Affective Disorder. Location is a very real factor. Law school demands three years of your life and untold hours of energy, concentration and hard work. If you get into Harvard and your spouse can't get a job in Massachusetts, you need to weigh the effect of this factor on your life.

Other factors to consider

If you already know you want to be a corporate lawyer you should review the transactional and corporate law options offered by each school you are considering. If a school is known for trial practice, make sure it offers the kind of transactional classes you think you need to take as well.

You might also study the breakdown of post-graduation placement. If a school places a large number of public interest lawyers or criminal justice attorneys in prosecutorial or defense positions, that school may not have all of the corporate law resources you may need. "Although I enjoyed my experience at the state university I attended," says one corporate associate, "it did not have what I would describe as a good corporate law program. The focus there was definitely on litigation practice. Most people there could not understand why I didn't want to take trial practice. When I told them that I intended never to go inside a courtroom, they looked at me like I was nuts. I was not able to take securities regulation because it was only offered every other semester. By the time I figured out that I needed to take it, it was too late." Be warned!

Making the Most of the Law School Experience

Corporate lawyers advise using the law school experience to get your first corporate law job, as well as how to decide whether corporate law is right for you.

"It's important to know how front-loaded law school is," cautions one second-year associate. "If you're into the standard track of working as a summer clerk at a medium or large firm with the goal of signing up with that firm upon graduation, then your first-year grades will be immensely important. That's because the hiring for 2L summer clerkships will be based almost entirely on your 1L successes. And turning that summer clerkship into a job upon graduation doesn't depend much at all on your 2L and 3L performance, since a law firm will make that decision on whether they like you or not during the summer. It's that 1L performance that puts you on track."

The two biggest mistakes you can make as a law student are falling behind in your work, and panicking about falling behind in your work. Make yourself a schedule, commit to it and treat your studying like it's a full-time job. In addition to studying, schedule in whatever you know keeps you sane – running, sitcoms, dinners with friends or family. Then, if you do fall behind, or if you feel like you're overwhelmed, find the right path back to balancing these two elements.

What classes should an aspiring corporate lawyer take?

At most law schools, your first year consists mostly, if not entirely, of required courses, including civil procedure, contracts, torts, criminal law and property. At some point in your law school career, you'll have to take a class on legal ethics and a legal writing course or a course on "lawyering" skills that includes writing. Some schools also require participation in moot court, which provides an opportunity to write briefs and prepare oral argument for an appeal.

Lawyers disagree on whether or how much your choice of courses will affect your career. "Don't take any class thinking it will help your practice of law," says one senior associate in a large Boston firm. "Nothing I learned in college – or for that matter law school – is particularly relevant to my day-to-day job. All learning in corporate practice is on the job. Take the classes that interest you in school – there's plenty of time for learning your job. I took tax, accounting, corporate law, secured transactions, but I think I would have been fine without all of them. I regret not taking international relations or other courses in their place." Steve McCormick, hiring partner at Kirkland & Ellis, never evaluates a prospective corporate associate based on the classes she takes. He does notice, however that the candidates who really want to go into corporate law do have a "complete exposure to mergers & acquisitions, venture capital and tax." "Business classes," he says, "are always helpful."

Some lawyers, particularly those who have made it to in-house positions, recommend as much exposure to business concepts and vocabulary as possible. Suggestions include contract drafting, corporations, securities, real estate or property law, capital markets, bankruptcy and secured transactions. The more you know about the substantive area of law you will practice, the easier your first several months of time-pressured associate life will be.

One in-house insider discourages students from taking "fluff classes." Instead, he recommends enrolling in real transactional classes that will help you understand how the business world works. "Take financial accounting and some sort of financial modeling class," says Daniel Boockvar, an in-house attorney at Weight Watchers International. "My one regret is that I didn't take these classes in law school. I wish I had studied the area where accounting meets financial planning and analysis. It would have been very helpful to already know how to budget, forecast and write a business case before I became so involved with a corporation's business decisions. I've worked hard to get up to speed."

Joint degrees in business: a mixed blessing?

An MBA is not necessary to secure work as a corporate associate, but joint degrees in law and business (JD/MBAs) have become increasingly popular in recent years. These degrees usually take four or more years to earn. Some require you to complete the first-year curriculum of both the law and business program in the first two years, and then allow you to take classes in each of the schools for the two remaining years.

Steve McCormick notes that, while not a prerequisite, a JD/MBA gives a prospective corporate lawyer "a huge advantage" in a law firm setting. Apparently the joint degree is of great advantage to an in-house corporate lawyer. "A joint JD/MBA is very useful if you want to go in-house," says the in-house counsel of a New York media company. "So much of my work is not just pure legal work – it's also understanding the business side and how the business side works. You're more valuable to your business colleagues if you have good business sense, and an MBA would be fantastic in giving you that. For example, if you have a good relationship with your sales people, a lot of time they'll ask you whether a deal makes sense to you. It's helpful if you can talk to them in a commercial sense and ask questions about pricing and the strategy of how to structure a deal. Business sense is also important when working with the M&A groups, since structure is so important to what they do."

A Boston law firm associate disagrees. "Unless your MBA is from Wharton, Harvard, Sloan or Columbia, don't bother; it won't help you. With MBAs there are only a handful of schools that carry any weight. Save your money and time – you can learn how to read financial statements on the job."

John DeRosa offers yet another perspective. "For a job search," he says, "both your law degree and your business degree have to come from top schools. But for actual work, a business background is always helpful. You'll not only be able to work on matters you might not otherwise be able to work on, but you'll also have a much better sense of why it has to be done, and what the client's goals are."

In the view of one JD/MBA graduate of University Pennsylvania Law School and Wharton Business School, "Some law firms have grown rather skeptical of JD/MBAs so in that sense the joint degree can be a disadvantage for pursuing a corporate law firm job. Many big law firms feel that JD/MBAs tend to leave sooner than other lawyers to pursue opportunities in business and finance, so their training investment is wasted."

Note that several large law firms in New York and other major cities give JD/MBAs an additional year's credit for purposes of seniority, pay and partnership qualification. In such firms, a JD/MBA would enter the firm as a second-year associate, as would a graduate who had spent a year completing a judicial clerkship. Check with prospective employers to negotiate seniority credit for an MBA.

Extracurriculars

Law review

Law review is a publication of scholarly legal articles produced by law students who compete for membership. Some schools will only admit students in the top 10 or 15 percent of the class. Many provide a "write-on" option (where admitance can be gained through winning a writing competition) or some combination of first-year grades and a writing sample. In the write-on, which usually takes place at the end of the first year, students are given a legal issue and a packet of sources and must put together an article, which will be judged by current law review members. Usually there are one or two competitive journals in a school and a few others that are open to all students. The big law firms that interview students at top schools know which journals are competitive and which are not.

Many employers rank law review and law journal experience as a high predictor of lawyering success. This experience signifies a certain proficiency in research and writing, skills essential to being a productive lawyer. "Journal membership is always a plus in interviews," says a Boston associate. "I think law review is particularly important if you are not coming from a top-10 school." A Florida in-house counsel agrees. "I think being on a law review or journal is a helpful addition to a resume for purposes of getting that first job, if not helpful in a practical sense." Moreover, the value of such journal experience goes beyond the initial interview. Law review has benefits even later in your career. Even employers who interview you for lateral positions will make a note that it's on your resume.

Clinics and other extracurricular activities

For corporate lawyers, more than for any other specialty, grades and law review trump everything else, so if you really want a career in corporate law, you shouldn't do anything at the expense of grades. But if you are able to balance your school workload with outside activities, legal aid clinics and other extracurricular activities can broaden both your resume and your world-view. And if you don't know whether you want to serve corporate clients or individuals with lower incomes, law school is a good time to find out.

If you aren't on a law journal, you can set yourself apart in interviews through your participation in legal aid clinics. Many students find clinic experience, in which law students under the supervision of faculty members offer free legal services to community members, valuable even though it usually involves litigation skills rather than corporate law skills. "I think my legal aid clinic experience was the most useful law-related activity even for my search for a corporate law job," says Sam Kim, an associate with a medium-sized Boston firm. "It actually gave me some practical experience that I could discuss with the interviewer. There are certain things every law student does to add credibility to his resume. Assuming that every law student is equally qualified, the difference is how you distinguish yourself in your resume and in person (interesting past jobs, non-academic recognition or achievements, clinics, and so on). These are things that will keep you in the interviewer's memory."

Other extracurricular activities can also help you impress an interviewer. Even if you know you don't want to be a litigator, moot court or trial competition experience can illustrate communications skills and the ability to perform under pressure and handle stressful situations. In fact, any kind of experience that shows you can manage stress well will work in your favor. Law firms recognize that it takes skills to have a leadership role in a student organization while handling a law student workload. This is not to say you should join every club at school – the key to using these activities to your advantage is to be very involved with one or two projects, and then to document that involvement well.

Summer Clerkships at Firms

While you're in law school, you have two "free" summers to stake a claim in a law firm as a summer clerk or associate.

Your first-year summer job

During their first summer, some students are able to land paid law firm jobs, but many others resort to unpaid internships in a variety of venues, including government or public interest work. "Take whatever legal job you can find, whether in a firm or the government or the public interest, or wherever," advises Cornell's DeRosa. "One-L legal jobs can be hard to come by so you may even need to take a non-paying legal job and then another non-law job to pay the bills. You can find these jobs through networking, reviewing job postings the career office collects for students or, for public interest work, at www.pslawnet.org [a public service law network] or www.idealist.org [home to hundreds of nonprofit job and internship listings]." "I did one summer at a public interest clearinghouse and one at a firm," says a law firm associate. "I would encourage everyone to spend their first summer at a public interest place to get an idea of what amazing work those underpaid and dedicated lawyers do. The summer I spent working there was an experience I'll always remember."

Cultivating professional relationships with law school professors is one way to get a job for your first summer. Employers often call respected faculty at their former law schools to ask for referrals to students who show promise in class. And many professors hire students to work as their research assistants. At the very least, professors will be able to write informed and enthusiastic letters of recommendation for students who take the time to impress them. At most, professors can help students get interviews for internships or jobs. Some top law firms offer internships specifically for minorities. You should certainly explore this option if it applies to you.

Be flexible

Tough economic times may mean that you have to take a summer job that's not everything you wanted. Some first-year students will indeed find legal jobs that fulfill many of their hopes and dreams. But many others will have to sacrifice something on their wish lists. Your goal for the summer should be to get some experience you can put on your resume as proof that you know how to analyze, research and write. If you are offered this kind of opportunity, albeit for lower pay or in a city you're not very excited about, you should take it. When a potential employer looks at your resume the next year, they're not going to know whether you got paid a cent. They will be reading about the experience you acquired.

Your second-year summer job

In their second summer during law school, most aspiring corporate lawyers compete to get offers for summer internships from the firms they want to work for after graduation. The interviewing process is almost exactly like the interviewing process for a permanent position. In many cases, it IS the same process, since most firms end up hiring a good portion of their summer class for permanent entry-level positions.

When you're talking about corporate law, you're talking about a market dominated by larger firms. And larger firms hire from on-campus interviewing programs and job fairs. Occasionally a firm will hire from a resume they receive in the mail, but usually they want to get as much of the hiring done through the on-campus interview process as possible. If they could hire all of their associates through the summer associate program, they would.

What kind of work can a corporate summer associate expect?

Firms run their summer associate programs differently. Some provide little to no structure, leaving a summer associate to use her own ambition to determine the kind of work she does. "If you spent the summer in Europe, what kind of experience would you have?" analogizes Kirkland & Ellis recruiting partner Steve McCormick. "It would depend on whether you visited 14 different countries or focused on one. At Kirkland, it's the same. We're not paternalistic; we let people chart their own course. They can choose whether to plunge into a deal or work on several different projects with different partners. I would hope that summer clerks get called on to stay until 3 a.m. when necessary, and that when they're called upon to do that, they do so, because the more they participate, the more they'll experience what it's like to be a full-time associate."

Other firms have a more structured summer associate program in place. Some require summer associates to rotate through more than one practice group, while others will ask you to choose an area of focus at the beginning of the summer. If you're not sure whether you want to be a transactional lawyer or a litigator, this can be a great opportunity to test things out. "Try to pick a firm that gives you a broad exposure over the summer," advises one tax associate. "That's how I ended up in my field. If you do stick with the firm, it is a great benefit to have had that wide exposure simply because you will know so many more of your co-workers."

Most associates speak positively of rotation programs. "I was able to rotate through litigation and through corporate during my summer clerkship, and it really helped me figure out that I didn't want to be a litigator," says a New York associate. "Litigation in a firm is much different from litigation in law school, where you're in front of a judge, in a courtroom and you're acting kind of like a Law and Order litigator, as opposed to litigation in a firm where you're writing memos in the background. I realized I enjoyed much more the corporate side of doing the documents. If you have the opportunity to try both kinds of practice, ask yourself how you feel about the litigation writing style. Do you like doing a lot of memos? Do you like doing a lot of writing in that style? I was tired of that. I was much more interested in going through a document and figuring out how the deal worked."

Despite McCormick's hope that the summer associate program gives students a real taste of law firm life, many associates think time as a summer associate doesn't present a realistic portrait. "Firms purposefully keep back the long hours from the summers, so you won't learn what it's really like to be an associate," says one lawyer. Your summer "may, however, give you an idea of what people you'd like to work more with in the firm or whether you want to do corporate or litigation or another practice area."

Will you get an offer?

Permanent associate positions really are getting more competitive. Fall 2001 summer programs resulted in 84 percent of summer clerks getting offers from NALP firms. That's down from 90 percent or more in preceding years.

The moral of the story is that you cannot take your summer internship for granted. Behave in a professional manner during your summer, and you will be asked back. The only expection? Some law firms, facing tough economic times, have recinded full time offers to summer interns. Make sure your summer employer is economically sound.

The Hiring Process

CHAPTER 5

Hiring Process Overview

Do you have to start your career at a large law firm?

Most corporate lawyers start at large law firms. Some work for government agencies, investment banks or exchanges, or corporations, but corporations typically hire lawyers with a few years of experience behind them. Even smaller firms tend to hire lawyers with some big firm experience. Easily 90 percent of students who want to practice corporate law go to firms of 100 or more attorneys. If you don't get a job with a large firm, you face a very small job market as a corporate lawyer.

"Given that corporate law is about transactions, the best place to get the most training is at a big corporate law firm" says Boockvar. "However, you can acquire relevant experience from government work at the SEC or the FTC [Federal Trade Commission] or any other government lawyer position that requires you review business transactions. Basically, if you don't start out in a corporate law firm, you have to distinguish between experience with the substance of a transaction and the process of a transaction. The substance consists of the commercial law and the terms of the commercial transaction. The process includes sourcing, due diligence negotiation, closing a deal and executing the deal. You can learn a lot about these process skills in other areas of the law. As a district attorney, you certainly learn to negotiate. As a commercial litigator, you probably learn to negotiate a settlement agreement. In a lateral job search, you need to stress those [skills]. You might say, 'I've negotiated 50 settlement agreements between corporations in litigation.' And if those settlement agreements involve commercial agreements, you can point out what you've learned about the substance of corporate law."

Still, big law firm experience is best for budding lawyers. "If your goal in corporate law is to be general counsel of a corporation, a couple of years of big firm experience will make you much more competitive," Boockvar explains. "The corporate decision-makers who have the power to hire you are looking for that. They aren't expecting you to have operating experience or even broad experience from this time as a big-firm corporate associate. They know you will only have narrow exposure to certain complicated merger and acquisition transactions, and maybe some exposure to corporate finance and securities. They know that these areas provide generalist insight into a lot of other areas, which is much more valuable and necessary for an in-house position than a specialization in ERISA or tax law."

Other than this substantive training, Boockvar sees two very important assets gained from big firm experience. "The first is discipline," he explains. "Surviving in a big firm means having the big firm work ethic beaten into you. If you embrace the expectations placed on you, you will leave the experience beaten but stronger. This prepares you for your life in a very demanding profession. It prepares you for having to work a lot of weekends and being at the beck and call of your clients and their investment bankers and other lawyers. When you go in-house this discipline can be a real asset when it's 7:00 and you think you're leaving work early, and you're the last one there other than the CEO. You've been trained to leave at 10:00 so when you leave at 7:00 you feel happy.

"The second advantage," Boockvar continues, "is the network available to you. When you get into a firm, meet as many people as you possibly can and make friends with as many people as you possibly can. Because it's one of the few times in your life that you'll have an instant network. You'll know between 400 and 600 people, each of whom will have connections in the business world. When I left my firm to join the internet startup Craftshop.com, I kept in touch with all of my colleagues and superiors at the firm, and when the company went bankrupt, those firm contacts got me my current job at Weight Watchers. And that's because I kept people up to speed on what I was doing."

Resumes

The first way employers will learn about all your fine qualities is through your resume. Facts are facts – but remember these rules of presentation.

Make your resume pleasing to the eye

Visual appearance is important – you don't want your resume too crowded or too sparse. You want it to be easy to read and skim through quickly. Assume that the person reading it is tired – if that person is a busy, successful corporate associate, it's a smart assumption to make. Don't make the font too small, and leave some white space on the page.

Draft it like a lawyer

Law firms expect the work of their associates to be error-free. If you have typographical errors in the one page you're using to represent yourself, how can a law firm trust you to produce an error-free 100-page transactional document under extreme time pressure? Remember that a spellchecker doesn't pick up everything. Proofread the resume yourself and enlist a few other people to proofread it as well.

Keep it to one page

Most law students should limit their resumes to one page. To warrant a second page, you need to have extensive work experience, and it needs to be really meaty stuff. Don't list every job you have ever held. Convey the most important information well. Your resume is another form of writing sample. If you express a five-word thought in 20 words, the person reading your application may worry about your ability to draft an agreement. Try to make descriptions interesting and captivating, but not over the top.

Highlight any business or corporate experience

If you can show a genuine interest in business or business law, highlight this on your resume. This experience can include anything from authoring a paper or law review article on a business law subject, to membership in a law school or bar associate corporate law association, to business credentials such as a CPA, CFA, securities license or real estate license.

Sample Resume, Courtesy of Cornell Law School Career Office

FIRST NAME LAST NAME

Email address
Current Address
Phone

Permanent Address
Phone

EDUCATION

HARVARD LAW SCHOOL, Candidate for J.D., May 2004

GPA 3.41 (Top 50%)

Activities Women's Law Coalition
Black Law Students Association
First Year Moot Court Competition

UNIVERSITY OF WISCONSIN, A.B. in Sociology, *magna cum laude*, June 2001

Honors: 4.0 Departmental Average
Scholarship for senior thesis research
Dean's List

Activities: Swim Team
Student Senate, Senior Class Representative
Women's Center Community Outreach Chairperson

EXPERIENCE

HON. SUSAN WILSON, U.S. DISTRICT COURT FOR THE DISTRICT OF RHODE ISLAND, Providence, R.I., Summer 2002

Judicial Intern Researched substantive and procedural issues, including elements of a RICO claim and joinder motion. Drafted memoranda, decisions, and orders on motions for summary judgment, reconsideration and default judgments. Observed and assisted in various aspects of trials, including drafting jury instructions and verdict sheets.

NATIONAL ORGANIZATION FOR WOMEN, New York, NY, Summer 2001

Policy Intern Staffed an information referral service for women dealing with domestic violence, rape, divorce, child custody, health care and employment issues. Wrote press releases. Drafted correspondence. Tracked pending legislation.

NEW YORK STATE GOVERNMENT SCHOLARS PROGRAM, New York, NY, Summer 2000

Intern Assisted the Language Service Coordinator of the Mayor's Office. Worked closely with city agencies in preparing, writing and researching a Language Community Services Mayoral Plan. Attended weekly seminars on state government.

LANGUAGES

Fluent in Spanish. Proficient in French.

REFERENCES

Vice Dean Jim Smith, Cornell Law School, phone number

Hon. Jill Jones, U.S. District Court for the District of Rhode Island, phone number

Assuming your resume is presentable, most employers look at your grades, the caliber of the institution from which you earned those grades, your ability to write and speak persuasively, and your interview performance.

Law School Grades

Law school grades are very important to your success as a lawyer. Earning high marks demonstrates the personal qualities that help to predict potential success as an attorney – attributes like motivation, goal orientation, productivity and the ability to concentrate. Large law firms, typically only consider a student whose grades are within a certain percentile, usually the top 5 to 20 percent of the class. For this reason, competition over grades can reach a fever pitch in law school. In a difficult market, grades become even more important. The firms who had a GPA cutoff of 3.4 from a highly ranked law school might raise that cutoff to 3.5 or 3.6.

Remember, however, that the large firm employers who look solely at grades aren't the only ones who will hire you to practice corporate law. And even those who have a grade cutoff are still looking for a way to distinguish among the many qualified law students who want those big firm jobs. "Fundamentally, I'm looking for two things," says Kirkland & Ellis's McCormick, "Strong analytical ability, and the ability to write and speak persuasively. Some firms, like ours, value self-reliance and self-motivation, someone who can go and figure things out on his own and seek out his own work, whether from partners and senior associates, or from new clients."

Even if your first-year grades are not in the top 20 percent of yor class, you might still be an attractive candidate for a lucrative, big firm job. You can set yourself apart from the crowd through law school activities, work experience in the real world or an upward trend in your grades. In fact, employers are often very impressed with an improved academic record. Low grades in the first year should not discourage anyone from attempting to excel through the remaining law school years. "I like people who've had a struggle along the way," says McCormick. "People who have it too easy have a hard time in real life."

But one law school career counselor voices a different perspective. "Nothing trumps grades for a big firm, not an MBA, not a proven interest in corporate law," he reports. "If you're at Harvard or Yale, grades matter less, since all employers will be willing to count the quality of your school in your favor. At any other premier school, grades are the deciding factor for a big-firm corporate law job. You don't need to show interest in corporate or business law if you're in the top half of the class. And this is true even in a down market."

Writing Samples and Transcripts

Some firms require you to submit a writing sample and a law school transcript before they'll even meet with you. To the extent you have something written for law school, you should use it. It should be well written, free of errors and fewer than 10 pages long. If you have questions about whether it is a good writing sample, discuss it with your legal writing instructor. If you are a second-year student, you may be able to use something from your summer internship, but you must get permission from your summer employer and redact any confidential information.

Most employers want to see something unedited, and they'll want to ask you questions about it. "You should pick a writing sample that you'll be able to talk about in an informed, impressive way," says DeRosa, "not just something that shows that you're a good writer. It's amazing how many times students are asked about their writing samples, and they have forgotten everything they wrote about. I tell them to prepare for their interview like it's a moot court argument."

(See the Appendix for an example of a law student's writing sample.)

Your Law School Career Office

All law school career offices provide print and online job listings and career information. Most provide individual counseling sessions to help you design your job search. Counselors can help you write or revise your cover letters and resumes and help you wade through the job listings they keep for students. Often, they run panels at which alumni share information about their own job searches and career paths. Some career offices connect students with graduates who can act as mentors, white others will videotape you in a mock interview to help you prepare for job interviews. "If the career office does mock interviews, that's a good idea," advises one Harvard grad. "First-years use the law school career office more because it's harder for them to get jobs. Once you're past the first year, if you had decent grades you don't need it as much, because everyone is coming to you."

Career services offices offer students a great deal more today than they did 20 years ago. The listings they provide are enormously varied and include government agencies, small firms, private companies, judges and public

National Association for Law Placement

The National Association for Law Placement (NALP) Guidelines promote the exchange of information and cooperation between law schools and employer. NALP serves as a source of information for legal career planning and recruitment. Law schools, law firms and other legal employers that are members follow certain standards for the timing of job offers and acceptances. These guidelines require that law firm offers be in writing and that candidates let other interested employers know when they accept an offer. The guidelines also limit the number of offers a student can hold open (thereby preventing another student from receiving an offer) at various intervals during the interviewing season.

NALP can be a great source of information about legal employers. In addition to extensive profiles of hiring policies and firm demographics, NALP also compiles surveys of associate compensation and other valuable information. For example, in a recent survey, NALP reported that median first-year associate salaries ranged from $53,500 in firms of two to 25 attorneys to $118,000 in firms of 500 attorneys or more. The median salary for all firms was $90,000.

interest organizations. One sign of a good career office is an effort to drum up business by calling on the alumni network. But develop a realistic sense of what the office can do for you. Your law school career office is not a headhunting firm. Counselors can provide all kinds of resources, but the legwork is still up to you. If you don't get a job through the on-campus interviewing and job fairs organized by the career office, you will have to do even more legwork. You will be responsible for submitting your resumes and getting your own interviews. If you don't get a job through on-campus interviewing, make your job search a priority. Use the career office regularly, and let the counselors who work there know what kind of job you're looking for. Make checking in with them a regular habit, just like going to class.

On-Campus Interviews

Law school career services offices usually organize a forum for on-campus interviews for summer clerkships and permanent positions. Usually, law firms are the employers interviewing on campus, but occasionally there are opportunities for an initial interview for a judicial clerkship, or, even more rarely, for an in-house legal position or business job. Usually, students will register for on-campus interviewing and submit their resumes to the career office, which will then forward the resumes to participating employers.

Each school runs on-campus interviewing (OCI) a bit differently. Some schools allow employers to screen resumes and decide whom they would like to interview, while others do not. In any event, students look at which employers are coming and, if they are interested in interviewing, they submit a resume. Sometimes interviews are given by lottery, and anyone who submits a resume can obtain an interview slot. In this system, employers distribute information about the type of candidate they hire, so students who don't have high enough GPAs won't even attempt to interview with them on campus.

A "cattle-call"

On-campus interviewing can be a valuable learning experience. It is sometimes the first time many students wear suits and learn how to sell themselves to a prospective employer. One associate remembers, "We submitted our resumes to the career office for the firms with which we wanted to interview. If the firm was interested in us, they would post our names on a sheet in the hall. We'd sign up for a time to meet with the firm on the day they came to interview." A second-year associate reflects more wryly on his experience, "On-campus interviewing is like a cattle-call. It offers the comfort of doing what everyone else is doing, but you get the idea that most of the law firms could sort most of the applicants without even talking to them."

According to a Harvard grad who has served as both interviewer and candidate, "The students who really impress you are those who sell you with their personality. If people aren't that interested in the job and they look bored, then the interviewer is going to feel like you're wasting their time. You don't want to do that, because even if you don't get or take this job, you never know where you'll run into this person in the future. Even if you have an iffier transcript, if you really sell yourself, when the interviewer goes back, they'll push for you that much more."

The goal of interviewing on campus is to be invited to a more in-depth interview at the law firm. This is a "callback" interview. "Callbacks involved traveling to the firm's office in another city. Usually that meant missing at least half a day of classes and study time," notes the same Harvard-trained lawyer. "After the callback, it might take the firm another month or so to let you know if you received an offer or not. A phone call usually meant an offer, and a letter usually meant a rejection."

Some students find the on-campus interviewing process stressful. "I ended up getting my first 'real' job through an on-campus interview, but the process itself at my school was extremely competitive," says a sixth-year associate. "Those few months during which I was interviewing for a summer clerk position were THE most stressful of my entire law school experience. Although I was lucky to get several interviews, the law firms that came on campus were only interested in seeing students in the top 20 to 25 percent of the class. So 75 to 80 percent of the students were not even getting interviews. This led to a lot of resentment among my classmates. (Not to mention that the interview and callback process is extremely time-consuming and interferes with classes and study time.) Ultimately, we all got jobs, but most people had to use methods other than the on-campus interview process."

In any kind of screening interview, you have a brief amount of time to impress the interviewer, sometimes as little as 20 minutes. Use that time to sell your strengths, even if it means turning around the questions you're being asked to get across the message you want to send about yourself. For example, if the interviewer asks, "What can I tell you about the firm?" you might answer with a short statement about who you are and what you might be able to do for a firm like theirs. You show your knowledge of, and interest in, the firm, and you have given the interviewer more information about yourself.

One associate who has been on the evaluation end of the process reminds students that the interview is your opportunity to flesh out the limited portrait offered by your resume and transcript: "At law firms, often you get the interview or callback interview because the employer is already satisfied with your paper credentials and thinks you're competent enough to do the job. Once you're in the door for the interview itself, try to make yourself human. Remember that the interviewing lawyers aren't trained human resources professionals; rather, they're evaluating you based on whether they think they'll want to work with you. Be human. Communicate your personality to them. Show self-awareness. And don't be afraid to tell a modest story or two, so long as it flows with the interview and is short!"

Skin-deep

When on-campus interviewing begins, about half of your classmates seem magically to know the rules for dressing for interviews. The other half of you try to eavesdrop on their conversations. For those who want a written source of information, here are some basic guidelines.

Law firms hire people who are professional and detail-oriented. The clothes you wear to an interview should reflect those qualities.

Men

Men should wear a conservatively cut, traditional two-button-style suit from the best designer they can afford (High quality shows high standards). Most of your classmates will choose navy blue suits, but black or gray is acceptable as well. Make sure that your socks match the color of your pants and that your shoes are polished. (Brown and black are equally good shoe color choices.) Under your jacket a crisp white shirt is the safest bet, and wear a tasteful tie with a simple pattern. Ask others if you're not sure you can recognize a tasteful tie. Try to get a good haircut several days before your interview.

Women

Women should wear a conservative navy or gray suit. Make sure the fit is not too tight, though the suit shouldn't be baggy either. Wear sheer pantyhose (preferably in a nude tone) and carry an extra pair in your briefcase or purse. Most women choose skirts that hit the knee, but some believe they will appear more professional if their skirts cover the backs of their knees. If in doubt, wear what makes you feel confident and professional. Wear a white or off-white silk shirt, preferably with a collar. The standard jewelry is a string of pearls and small pearl earrings. If your hair is longer than shoulder length, put it back. Don't paint your nails red. Wear basic black or navy pumps with one to two inches of heel.

Both men and women should wear a dress watch and carry a real leather briefcase. If weather is poor, you should try to wear a dress overcoat or trench coat and carry a classy, full-size umbrella rather than a cheap disposable umbrella you picked up in a drugstore. Help your interviewer picture how you would look to a client. Convey the image that you've been dressing up and dealing with moneyed corporate executives all your life.

Off-Campus Interviews and Callbacks

During an on-campus interview, you will meet with one or two people for a short period of time. In a callback interview, or any other kind of formal law firm interview, you meet with several attorneys, sometimes as many as six or seven, and spend most of the day at the firm. The interviews are usually broken up with a lunch, which is an interview in and of itself. About half of all callback interviews result in offers of employment, which is down from 63 percent in prior years.

"I like to start by asking about the candidate's core academic experience," explaines Kirkland & Ellis recruiting partner Steve McCormack. "I like people with success in text analysis and writing, whether on law review or somewhere else." Some lawyers (often those with fantastic grades who ultimately received lots of job offers) remember the process fondly. "Callback interviews were fun," says one associate, "My chance to ask a lot of honest questions about the place and honestly answer their questions." Associates with experience as both interviewer and interviewee explain the object of the interview. "Firm interviews are not very staged," says one senior associate who's done her share of interviewing for her firm. "The interviewer is just trying to figure out if you're the kind of person he or she could leave alone with clients and, in addition, the kind of person he or she would want to have a beer with when the day is done. The best interviewees can have a relaxed conversation."

The rules that apply to other kinds of interviews apply to law firm interviews as well. Be early, but not too early. Be courteous to everyone you meet, from the receptionist to the hiring partner. Be engaging, enthusiastic and interested. Avoid any appearance of arrogance. Show that you really want the job. Don't get so nervous that you appear stiff or bored or uninterested. Don't ask inappropriate questions. One young associate who interviews candidates offers these specific cautions: "You should appear seriously interested in the job. You should tell your story well, whatever it is. Don't come across as a personality zero. Take an interest in the interviewer. Never hedge or be defensive – be open and excited." Nevertheless, warns another lawyer, "Remember that the interviewers are not your friends. Don't kick back and say things that you'd say to your friends, but not to a partner at a firm."

Before going to an interview, look up the firm's web site and note where the attorneys are from and what schools they went to so you can chat about anything you might have in common. During conversational lulls ask questions to keep the conversation going: how long they have been at the firm, what they do, and so on.

If you have too many firm interviews in a short period of time, the biggest challenge might be stamina. According to a seven-year law firm veteran, "At Harvard, we had a 'fly-out week,' during which we didn't have any classes and were expected to leave for interviews. We scheduled all our interviews for one or two locations, and flew out and stayed in a hotel. I was doing maybe two interviews a day, meeting with five people per firm. This is a lot more tiring than an on-campus interview, because you have to go at it again and again, and you have to think of new questions for these people so you seem interested. Interviews are all about personality, especially when they take place at the law firm, because the people interviewing you often don't have your grades. They're looking at how enthusiastic you are, how interested you are and whether you can relate to your interviewer."

In short, be yourself! You only have a short time to determine if you would fit in with that firm's environment. If you are not comfortable with where you work, you most likely will not be as happy and successful as you could be.

Avoid this interviewing mistake!

The most egregious mistake a prospective associate can make on her interview is to show a lack of curiosity about the firm. Strangely, it's also the most common mistake. "At the end of the interview, I always ask if they have any other questions," says one interviewer. "If they say they don't have any questions, I know they're not really interested in making sure they're a good fit. Basically, the name of the institution ends the analysis – they have no interest in the firm beyond the name, so they can tell their parents and their friends they work at XYZ law firm. And they get this from law schools. Law schools fall into the same trap, so they don't teach curiosity to their graduates. The idea that big firms are fungible is just laughable."

Associates agree. "Be sure to have at least 10 to 15 questions about the firm and about the work they do or about the position for which you are interviewing ready to ask the interviewer. There will always be an opportunity to ask questions and it looks really bad if you don't have any questions prepared," says one associate.

"Don't lose sight of fact that you are interviewing for a job," warns a hiring partner. "Students tend to deify law firms and forget that they're employers. The elephant in the room is the money the law firm is offering to the associate. Firms are particularly sensitive about that money, so they want you to be able to come up with another reason you're interested in the firm. Even just saying that you have talked to one associate at the firm or that you've studied the firm web site can make a big difference."

In 2002, law firm hiring took a nosedive. The number of job offers made to 2Ls who got callback interviews fell from 63 percent in 2000 to 51 percent in 2001, according to NALP, and many experts feared this year's recruiting season would bring another big drop. So far, that doesn't appear to be the case. If you are looking in a weak market, you may have to work even harder to impress your interviewer. One premier law school career counselor has cautioned that finding a corporate law position is significantly harder than finding almost any other kind of position. He counsels students to pick another area if they have any interest in it. If corporate is what they really want, he advises them to read the business sections of *The Wall Street Journal* and *The New York Times* daily for three months before the interview.

Sample Interview Questions

1. What got you interested in the law?
Try to pick a concrete personal experience, either academic or practical, that led to your interest or reinforced it.

2. What did you do last summer?
Whatever you did, whether it was legal work or a summer course or non-legal work, talk up the transferable skills you acquired. If you did legal research and writing for a judge, talk about how nice it was to apply your law school skills to real world problems. Even if you helped out in the family restaurant business, talk about how you were exposed to the basics of running a business and how it gave you a perspective on the role of a business lawyer.

3. How did you like law school?
The same principles apply to this question. Think of something to say about your law school experience that is concrete and positive and adds to the good impression you are already building in the interviewer's mind.

Occasionally, you will get a lawyer who will ask standard questions like "Where do you see yourself in five years?" "What are your best qualities?" "What are your worst qualities?" "If you were a tree, what kind of tree would you be?" and so on. These may seem like ridiculous questions, and many interviewers won't ask them. Even so, be prepared with good answers just in case. The most important thing is to answer with good humor and a good attitude. Don'y become irritable or defensive.

Interview Follow-Up

Our mothers always tell us to follow up invitations with a thank you note. Career services offices say the same thing about interviews. But do employers really notice?

One associate suggests that a follow-up strategy may be worth your time. "Writing a follow-up note may not make a difference for a law firm interview, but it can't hurt either. It is especially nice for on-campus interviewers, because they really are trying to make a decision about whether to ask you back to the firm." On the other hand, Sam Kim confides, "I don't think I did any follow-up. Then again, I think the market was a lot better for entry-level attorneys. Honestly, when I interview prospective candidates and I get a follow-up letter, I may skim it and quickly discard it. It does not make much difference in my recommendation to hire or not, since I've already filled out my views on such candidate right after the interview and turned it in."

"Sometimes I wrote thank you notes," says Kathy Hartland, an in-house counsel with six years of law firm experience, "but I never found this to be necessary. As an interviewer, if someone sent me a note and spelled my name wrong or got something wrong (made a typo or anything) that person received black marks. If someone failed to send a note, I never noticed. A better thing to do," she suggests, "would be to call the firm if you haven't heard from them after about a month if you are a law student, or a couple weeks if you are a lateral. Chances are that you did not get the job, but it may be that the firm just hasn't decided if they need a new employee or not. By calling them and making a polite inquiry, a candidate can remind the firm that they really do need someone and should make a decision."

Troubleshooting

What if you don't get a job through on-campus interviewing?

If you don't get a job through an on-campus interviewing process, there is still hope. Make an appointment with a counselor in your career services office to talk about what might have gone wrong and to do some mock interviewing to hone your skills. One advantage of your situation is that you can now target firms and locations for reasons other than that THEY chose YOU! Now's your time to think about where you want to live and what kind of firm would give you the best combination of worklife and money.

If you're not attending law school in the region where you want to practice, things are a little trickier. Book a flight for your spring break to the city, or one of the cities, in which you'd like to practice. Get a list of the alumni from your law school and your college who practice law in that city. Then contact these alumni. Usually, a letter and a follow-up phone call work best. Don't try to get a job from these people – just ask for an informational interview. Tell them you want to ask their advice about the job market and legal community in their city. If they like you, you can be sure they'll let you know if their firm has an opening for you, and will keep you in mind when they hear about other openings. Once you have a few of these informational interviews set up, you can write to all the firms with corporate law departments in that city. Tell them that you would like to meet them to talk about job opportunities and that you will be in that city for an interview during the week of your choice.

Research other employers. Look for alumni at those firms with whom you can network. Some research tools include Martindale-Hubbell (www.Martindale.com), the NALP Directory of Legal Employers (www.nalpdirectory.com) and local bar associations. "In this situation you might also need to assess where you are looking and what types of employers you are looking at – and potentially expand your search to other geographic regions or other employers," advises John DeRosa. "OCI only brings in a small number of all of the legal employers that are in the world," he explains, so students "should start doing some research and networking to see where else they can apply. It helps to set a goal each week, such as, 'This week I will contact five networking contacts and try to drum up some leads for openings' or 'I will mail out 10 cover letters and resumes.'"

Networking

Even if all the doors in the world are open to you and you have no problem getting interviews, networking can still be useful. Talking to corporate lawyers, or people who know corporate lawyers, about what they do can be a great way to educate yourself about your chosen career. Networking for example, can provide a valuable source of information to help you ask the right questions and intelligently assess whether a firm is right for you.

Moreover, networking can be a great way to hear about a job opening that may not be known to the general public or to get an edge on the competition where the candidates are otherwise equally qualified. You can network with law school friends who already have job offers, as well as both law school and undergraduate alumni. But don't stop there. If you have trouble finding the kind of job you want, you should network with everyone you know.

"Networking is important for lateral moves," notes one associate. "If you are considering a move once you're in practice, tell everyone you know you're looking. I ended up at this firm because a friend's uncle suggested they were hiring." Sam Kim agrees. "Networking in any context is very, VERY, VERY important. I know that there's a stigma attached to it – slimy, brown-nosing, desperate. However, networking includes relationships you build throughout your life in social, academic and professional contexts. The best recommendations and connections came from those who got to know me personally through my relationships with them – friends, colleagues, military buddies, my military superiors, co-workers, partners, and so on."

"Even if you have great credentials," says in-house counsel Kathy Hartland, "having someone you know make a quick phone call for you can make a huge difference. And most of the time, [your coworkers] are very glad to do that for you. At the very least, it can help you get your foot in the door. If the person interviewing you knows someone you know, that can be a big help in getting the job. The interviewer only has a few minutes to assess your personality – but a good reference can provide the interviewer with the comfort he or she needs to go ahead and hire you. It's not essential, but it definitely gives you an edge. Depending on the job market, it can be very helpful. I understand that when you are starting out, it's hard to use 'connections' to get a job, especially in a city where you don't know anyone. Be creative and think hard about who you know and who could put in a good word for you. Talk to everyone about your job search: your dentist, your hairdresser, your neighbors, your parents' friends, and so on."

As in many other settings, the best way to establish a networking relationship is by asking people to talk about themselves and what they do. "In a legal market where there is so much competition, the vast majority of better jobs are never advertised," notes DeRosa. Unless you build a network to tap into jobs your career office may not know about, you'll be facing a much more limited job search. Attending meetings of your local bar association can be an easy way to network. Show up at a corporate law committee meeting. Your first visit might be uncomfortable, but you don't have to do anything other than introduce yourself. You'll see the same people every month, and eventually you'll be able to talk to them about what they do. They'll keep you in mind for future jobs and internship opportunities.

Networking is good for getting both jobs and clients. When a firm or a client is looking for an attorney they are going to ask other attorneys, or people who know other attorneys. So the more people who know you, the better chance you have. You are selling yourself and your services to others.

How can you overcome poor grades?

Some people who might be excellent lawyers in the future just don't do well in law school. If you're one of those people, and you're committed to pursuing a career in corporate law, you might despair when you look at the grade cutoffs for many firms. How can you overcome poor grades in a job search?

One way is to develop excellent interviewing skills and the ability to talk about your academic performance in a non-defensive manner. Explain your situation briefly and end on a positive note. For example, point out something on your resume or transcript you feel is more indicative of your abilities than the low grades. Be creative in your job search. If employers aren't coming to you, go to them. Follow all the networking strategies discussed above. Think about interning with a large corporation for the summer, even in a semi-legal capacity. Occasionally, a large corporation will recommend such a person to its primary law firm. One law school placement officer suggests that students approach the overseas branch of a law firm for a temporary position. Sometimes this can help you find a job with the firm's U.S. counterpart.

If you've just received your first-year grades and know that you're not competitive with other job seekers, put every effort into your school's legal writing competition and get onto law review. If an interviewer sees that you were on law review, she might assume you have grades high enough to merit membership and not ask for your transcript. In any case, being on law review is impressive enough to get you in despite your GPA.

Consider other options

If you do have weak grades, DeRosa advises that you ask some hard questions. "Is it realistic to think that you'll overcome them? If you're in your third year, and your grades are problematic, you'll probably not be successful in finding a corporate law job, because you can't overcome grades entirely. If your grades are borderline, journal experience, moot court or a well-focused elective coursework track can make a difference. If the professor at your law school who's most known for corporate law can write a recommendation for you, that can make a difference. Those are cases where the student's grades are below the line, but not enormously so."

Many students with lower grades will have better luck getting jobs in a different legal specialty. If a student hasn't found a job through on-campus interviewing, he should determine what drew him to corporate law in the first place, and consider whether commercial litigation, tax, commercial real estate or bankruptcy might be an attractive alternative. Lastly, bear in mind that there are opportunities to practice corporate law outside large firms in the private sector. Aspiring corporate lawyers typically don't picture themselves in government agencies like the SEC or a state attorney general's office that administers state securities ("blue sky") laws, but these are alternatives to law firm practice that weigh grades less intensively than the private sector.

What if you graduate without a job?

Your first priority is to make sure you are not distracted from bar preparation. If you don't have a job and you fail the bar exam, redouble your efforts and pass it the next time it is offered. Keep the energy you expend in a job search to a minimum. After you pass the bar, make a pest of yourself with your career office and any employers you decide to target. At that point, you should follow the same advice as those students with lower grades in refocusing your job search.

The Bar Exam

During the first semester of your third year, you will register for a state bar exam. Depending on the state, this is a two- or three- day exam that tests substantive legal knowledge. It is usually a combination of multiple choice, short answer and essay questions. In addition, virtually all states require practicing attorneys to pass the Multi-State Professional Responsibility Exam (MPRE), which may be taken during the fall or spring of your third year or in August following the bar examination. You must pass this multi-state examination in order to be licensed even if you have passed the state bar examination given in late July or February. Some states require you to take the MPRE before you take the bar exam. Even if this is not true of your state, keep in mind that you cannot be admitted to the bar until you take this test.

In the past, you could only practice law in the state in which you passed the bar, no matter how many years of experience you had as a lawyer. Only a few states, like Montana and the District of Columbia, would allow you to apply for a waiver. Recently, the American Bar Association has made an effort to change this. Under the new Model Rule on Admission by Motion, no additional bar exam would be required of lawyers who hold a degree from an ABA-accredited law school, have passed a state bar and have practiced law for five of the seven preceding years. Although individual states are free to restrict lawyers in whatever way they see fit, they typically abide by ABA rules.

Leading Employers and Recruiters

CHAPTER 6

How does Vault come up with its rankings? The first step is to compile a list of the most renowned law firms in the land by reviewing the feedback we receive from previous surveys, consulting our previous lists, poring over legal newspapers, talking to lawyers in the field and checking out other published rankings. This year, our initial list was made up of 148 law firms. We asked the firms to distribute a password-protected online survey to their associates. In total, 11,908 attorneys returned anonymous surveys to Vault. We heard from lawyers in New York, Los Angeles, San Francisco, Palo Alto, Chicago, Boston, Philadelphia, Houston, Dallas, Washington, D.C., Miami, Cleveland, Seattle, Orlando, Phoenix and Atlanta, among many other U.S. locations, not to mention London, Paris and beyond. The online survey asked attorneys to score each of the law firms on a scale of 1 to 10 based on how prestigious it is to work for the firm. Associates were asked to ignore any firm with which they were unfamiliar and were not allowed to rank their own firm.

Think it's easy getting 11,908 associates to take our survey? Think again. Lawyers are busy people, and many are stressed out as it is without having to take 30 minutes out of their day to work on a non-billable project – especially with the increased emphasis on racking up billable hours. Despite it all, an incredible amount of associates came through for us and helped us produce the Vault rankings. Associates, many thanks for your insight and patience.

For the departmental rankings, associates were allowed to vote for up to three firms in their practice areas and were not permitted to vote for their own firm. Associates who identified themselves as corporate attorneys were only allowed to vote in corporate-related categories (securities, business finance, etc.); litigators were only allowed to vote in the litigation category, and so on. We indicate the top firms in each area, as well as the total percentage of votes cast in favor of the firm. (Each associate surveyed chose three firms; the maximum percentage of votes per firm is 33.3 percent.)

Top Ranked Corporate Employers

RANK	FIRM	% OF VOTES	2003 RANK
1	Cravath, Swaine & Moore LLP	18.53	1
2	Wachtell, Lipton, Rosen & Katz	14.54	3
3	Skadden, Arps, Slate, Meagher & Flom*	14.39	2
4	Sullivan & Cromwell LLP	11.38	4
5	Davis Polk & Wardwell	8.19	5
6	Simpson Thacher & Bartlett	5.45	6
7	Cleary, Gottlieb, Steen & Hamilton	3.57	7
8	Shearman & Sterling	2.41	8
9	Latham & Watkins LLP	2.26	9
10	Weil, Gotshal & Manges LLP	1.63	NR

Source: Vault Guide to the Top 100 Law Firms, 2004 Edition
** Skadden, Arps, Slate, Meagher & Flom LLP and Affiliates*

#1 - Cravath, Swaine & Moore LLP

Ms. Lisa A. Kalen
Associate Director of Legal Personnel and Recruiting
Phone: (212) 474-3215
Fax: (212) 474-3225
E-mail: lkalen@cravath.com

#2 - Wachtell, Lipton, Rosen & Katz

Ms. Elizabeth F. Breslow
Director of Recruiting and Legal Personnel
Phone: (212) 403-1334
Fax: (212) 403-2334
E-mail: recruiting@wlrk.com

#3 - Skadden, Arps, Slate, Meagher & Flom LLP and Affiliates

Ms. Carol Sprague
Director of Legal Hiring
Phone: (212) 735-3815
Fax: (917) 777-3815
E-mail: csprague@skadden.com

#4 - Sullivan & Cromwell LLP

Ms. Nicole Adams
Assistant Manager of Legal Recruiting
Phone: (212) 558-3518
Fax: (212) 558-3588
E-mail: adamsn@sullcrom.com

#5 - Davis Polk & Wardwell

Ms. Bonnie Hurry
Director of Recruiting & Legal Staff Services
Phone: (212) 450-4144
Fax: (212) 450-5548
bonnie.hurry@dpw.com

#6 - Simpson Thacher & Bartlett

Ms. Dee Pifer
Director of Legal Employment
Phone: (212) 455-2687
Fax: (212) 455-2502
E-mail: dpifer@stblaw.com

#7 - Cleary, Gottlieb, Steen & Hamilton

Mr. Jaime E. Martinez
Manager of Legal Recruitment
Phone: (212) 225-3163
E-mail: jmartinez@cgsh.com

#8 - Shearman & Sterling

Ms. Suzanne Ryan
Manager, Professional Recruiting
Phone: (212) 848-4592
Fax: (212) 848-7179
E-mail: sryan@shearman.com

#9 - Latham & Watkins LLP

Ms. Debra Clarkson
701 B Street, Suite 2100
San Diego, CA 92101
Phone: (619) 236-1234
E-mail: debra.clarkson@lw.com

#10 - Weil, Gotshal & Manges LLP

Ms. Donna J. Lang
Manager of Legal Recruiting
Fax: (212) 735-4502
E-mail: donna.lang@weil.com

Legal Recruiter Directory

AMERICAN Legal Search, LLC

100 Park Avenue
16th Floor
New York, NY 10017
Phone: (212) 984-1086
Fax: (212) 880-6439
www.americanlegalsearch.com
Rhonda K. Singer, Esq., Managing Director
rhonda@americanlegalsearch.com

AMERICAN LEGAL SEARCH
Where Lawyers Look for Lawyers

AMERICAN Legal Search, LLC is a full-service national legal search firm. Before launching AMERICAN, our executive management team founded and built one of the largest privately held legal search firms in North America. From law firm mergers and practice group acquisitions to permanent search and contract staffing, AMERICAN's principals have been serving the legal communities throughout the country for more than a decade.
AMERICAN operates three core business divisions:

1. Assist law firms with firm mergers, practice group acquisitions and expansions into new cities.
2. Placement of associates and partner-level lawyers with law firms and corporations on a permanent basis.
3. Placement of contract (temporary) attorneys for specific projects.

Conduit Recruiting Corp.

145 West 45th Street
8th Floor
New York, NY 10036
Phone: (212) 768-2121
Fax: (212) 768-2821
www.conduitrecruiting.com

Mark P. Arrow
President
Phone: (212) 768-2121
arrow@conduitrecruiting.com

conduit

Take this job, and love it !

Conduit Recruiting Corp. is a leading legal recruiting firm that places legal professionals with national and international law firms and corporations. Each Conduit client and candidate benefits from our commitment to personalized attention, customized searches and innovative technology - the cornerstones of our business. We are dedicated to fostering partnerships with our clientele to ensure mutually beneficial matches. With our dynamic client base and access to high-caliber candidates, Conduit connects people to jobs.

Kass-Abell & Associates, Inc.

Kass/Abell & associates
Attorney Placement

10780 Santa Monica Blvd.
Suite 200
Los Angeles, CA 90025
Phone: (310) 475-4666
Fax: (310) 475-0485
www.kassabell.com

Peter J. Redgrove, President
Phone: (310) 475-4666
attyplcmnt@kassabell.com

Kass Abell & Associates has 22 years of experience successfully conducting searches for corporate law departments and law firms in California. Our team of experienced recruiters take great pride in representing the needs of clients and candidates in an ethical and professional manner. Peter Redgrove's reputation as a leader in the IN-HOUSE sector is widely acknowledged. Our LAW FIRM representation includes leading firms in Los Angeles, Orange County, San Diego, San Francisco and Silicon Valley.The success of Kass Abell is based on our caring Commitment to every search we undertake.

We a founding member of NALSC.

Myra Binstock Legal Search.

121 Squire Hill Road
Upper Montclair, NJ 07043
Phone: (973) 783-6006
Fax: (973) 783-0037
www.myrabinstock.com

Myra Binstock
President
Phone: (973) 783-6006
Fax: (973) 783-0037
myrab2@aol.com

Myra Binstock Legal Search is a goal-oriented search firm whose principal is dedicated to hands-on counseling and personal involvement in introducing those people who will work best together. Whether the applicant is an entry-level attorney or a seasoned professional, each is given ample time and attention to productively focus on their career path. Myra is a former paralegal whose own career includes years both as an administrative assistant to an Appellate Division Judge and sole paralegal for a Fortune 100 corporation. She understands the working environment of companies and law firms, and knows how to match the right person to the job.

The Legal Recruiters Inc

275 Madison Avenue
Suite 612
New York, NY 10016
Phone: (212) 856-4412
Fax: (212) 880-4246
www.thelegalrecruiters.com

Muriel Wolland, President
Phone: (212) 856-4412
info@thelegalrecruiters.com

Placing attorneys since 1986 in corporations, financial institutions and law firms, in legal, quasi-legal and non-legal positions.

Placement specialties: corporate/securities (with a sub-specialty in structured finance, structured products, and securitization), international, banking/bank regulatory, M&A, tax, ERISA, labor/employment, intellectual property, insurance, and environmental.

In-house clients include financial conglomerates, bulge bracket investment banks, commercial banks, rating agencies, credit enhancers, broker/dealers, hedge funds, issuers, consulting firms, and manufacturing/consumer products.

Law firms, both domestically and internationally, range from NYC-based to branches and boutiques, and non-US based firms; placements in the tri-state area, as well as coast-to-coast and throughout Europe and Asia.

The PeterSan Group

270 Madison Avenue
15Th Floor
New York, New York 10016
Phone: (212) 981-4500
Fax: (212) 981-4560
www.Petersan.com

THE PeterSan GROUP
LEGAL SEARCH CONSULTANTS

Sandrea Friedman, Esq., Peter Goldfeder, Peter Gosule
Managing Directors
Phone: (212) 981-4500 | E-mail: Petersan@nyct.net

The PeterSan Group places attorneys in all areas of expertise as associates, partners, in-house counsel and general counsel and in business and non-legal positions. We also represent law firms in the acquisition of practice groups and firm mergers. Searches are conducted on a retainer or contingency fee basis.

Our clients include leading law firms worldwide as well as financial institutions, investment banks, consumer product, health care, pharmaceutical, entertainment and other Fortune 500 companies.

We work closely with our clients to establish a comprehensive understanding of the particular needs of every search. We then conduct each search in a highly confidential and professional manner.

ON THE JOB

The Work

CHAPTER 7

Starting Your New Career

You have just spent three years of your life learning the law. You were recruited by a law firm offering you a big salary, challenging work and the possibility of partnership in the future. You have a new suit and a sleek new briefcase. You feel good. You receive your first project from your supervising partner. You suddenly realize you know absolutely nothing

Don't panic. This is when you need to recognize that being successful as a lawyer requires the same skills as being successful at anything. You have to ask questions, work hard and be diligent. If you do this, you will succeed. There is nothing magical about the legal profession. Like most jobs, it requires your all in order to excel. Unlike most other jobs, your "all" is required in the office more than 40 hours per week (more like 60). Remember, there are reasons for the big salary. Don't fool yourself into thinking otherwise.

There is a good reason why recruiting partners like to see real world work experience on a resume. No one's saying that college and law school aren't stressful or challenging experiences. But there's something different about the kind of stress integral to a full-time job in a service-oriented industry. While before, as a student, you were the only one who would suffer or prosper from your own work, now there are clients depending on you. And before your work gets to a client, it usually passes under the scrutiny of senior associates and partners who must take responsibility for the work you do. In fact, the whole money-making structure of a law firm is based on the idea that an associate will put in a certain number of hours of work which will be billed at a much higher rate than that associate will see in the form of her paycheck. No client would pay a partner's rate for hours and hours and hours of legal research, but that research has to be done, and the partner has to take responsibility for it.

Training and orientation

The amount of training and orientation you will receive depends on the size of the firm and the circumstances of your hiring. If you are hired for a summer clerkship, much of your training and orientation will happen during that time. If you're hired later, after you graduate or after a year at another firm or in another discipline, your training will take place then.

At any firm, someone will show you around the office, explain the computer and phone systems, teach you how to bill your time and tell you where to find the firm law library and other research tools. At most large firms, there are enough new associates joining the firm at the same time to merit an organized, intensive training and orientation. Such firms might have seminars or discussions on drafting transaction documents, client service, legal research, marketing, management, financial planning, negotiation skills and other nuts and bolts of an associate's practice. A few law firms, recognizing the gap between law school education and what it takes to be a lawyer, provide further training in client expectations, partner expectations, ethics, technology, life/work balance, how to make partner, leadership and basic law firm economics.

The work of a junior corporate associate

Part of your first year as a corporate associate at a big firm involves learning to be a glorified secretary. It will be your responsibility to keep all documents organized, to schedule meetings and to send out copies of pertinent documents to all parties involved. You're often responsible for other grunt work as well, like faxing, Fedex-ing, copying and proofreading. If you are starting your first job, you may have to learn the hard way exactly how to communicate with partners and senior associates, juggle assignments, get along with your co-workers and delegate assignments to paralegals and secretaries.

A new associate will have substantive work beyond the "grunt work" and socialization. Most of this work can be broken down into a few different categories: due diligence, research and writing of memoranda, and drafting documents and preparing filings for state and federal agencies. Some junior associates spend all of their time on research projects. Others proofread documents for weeks at a time. Most associates also receive a great deal of training and mentoring from partners or senior associates on the other aspects of a corporate law practice. Drafting contracts, corporate resolutions and securities disclosure statements are not skills typically learned in law school, so there is a great deal of trial and error. Most law firms have extensive files of similar documents to which you can refer. It's rare that you will be asked to draft anything from scratch.

There's not a lot of time for intellectual curiosity at this stage of your career. Your superiors will give you specific assignments that must be completed immediately. Someone else has usually thought through the bigger issues and wants you either to confirm what he or she already thinks (if you are to research something) or to proofread a document for internal consistency. Many lawyers note that the training you receive in law school, which is heavy on case law and drafting research memoranda, doesn't really prepare you for the work of a practicing corporate attorney. A junior associate in Philadelphia claims to have read only a handful of cases and written very few research memos since joining the firm. Another associate observes, "Good corporate lawyers have a sense of what the business world requires and don't get caught up in legal minutia, although good law students are supposed to enjoy wallowing in such details."

How do you get your work?

Many lawyers breathe a sigh of relief when they hear new associates are on the way, and immediately start hoarding research projects, planning to recruit the new bloood for proofreading and other tasks. At some firms, there are no obstacles to your direct and immediate relationship with these people. You can plunge right in and bill lots of hours right away. You will learn by doing and can ask questions of more senior associates along the way.

Some firms put one or two lawyers in charge of the summer clerks or new associates, and those lawyers monitor your work schedule. They might try to make sure every new associate gets to work with several different lawyers. Some might ask about your interests and tailor your work to those interests when possible. They might even assign you a mentor who can help you when you get stuck and offer advice for handling assignments. Don't take on so much work that you can't get it done accurately, but don't turn down work just so you can leave after an eight-hour day. If you see everyone else working a 12-hour day, you should expect to work those hours as well.

It's very likely that in your first year or two you will feel overwhelmed at times. According to one junior associate, the unpredictability of a corporate lawyer's schedule – slow, leisurely days filled with Internet surfing and ending at 5 p.m., followed by intense, high-pressure days lasting till 5 a.m. – is "the hardest thing to get a handle on." Even if there is no formal mentoring system, it's a good idea for new associates to find someone more senior whom they can turn to for advice and support. Francesca Lavin, a seventh year associate in New York and a mentor to first-years at Cleary Gottlieb, notes that no firm likes to see its associates unhappy and suggests that "instead of just resigning yourself to your first couple of years being crazy," you should find someone you can talk to when you are in over your head.

Job Responsibilities

Due diligence

Due diligence, also called document review, is the process of reviewing existing legal and business contracts of a business (including corporate documents, agreements and financial statements) for potential problems and issues prior to a proposed transaction, such as a merger or acquisition. The usual goal is to make sure that there is nothing in any of the contracts that would prohibit the sale of the company (or require a third party's consent) and to make sure that the contract will not terminate as a result of the sale. Usually, an associate will catalog the documents he or she has reviewed and write summaries of the key agreements. For example, when a merger is being considered and the acquirer hasn't had the time to read all of the contracts of the company it is considering purchasing, the lawyers will be expected to summarize the agreements. The purpose of due diligence is to give your client the clearest possible picture of the company you're examining, so the client can assess the risks and benefits of going through with the contemplated transaction.

In an initial public offering, due diligence involves reading agreements that are summarized in the deal prospectus – the document given to prospective investors summarizing important information about the company and the deal – to make sure the prospectus is correct. If you are representing an underwriter in a securities offering, you will review documents so that the underwriter can claim to have made a reasonable investigation of the issuer's statements in the offering document. Basically, it's done so that the underwriter will be able to claim the due diligence defense if there is a material misstatement in the offering document. ("I investigated and everything looked fine, so don't come after me with a lawsuit because the investors lost their money.")

A junior associate does more due diligence than contract drafting because one of the best ways to learn to draft contracts is to read a lot of them. In the past, lawyers frequently traveled to the company they were reviewing and reviewed all the materials pertinent to the transaction on site. Some attorneys have noticed a trend toward cutting back on lawyer travel. Apparently, clients have discovered it's cheaper to have their own employees copy all the documents and send them to the law firm for review.

If you do travel to the company, document review is a sure way to bill a lot of hours in a short period of time. You won't have the luxury of wasting time looking for work or trying to decide whether to go to lunch with your colleagues. And no one can give you any non-billable work to do, like updating the firm's research files. The company sets aside a room for you and puts all the documents in there, and you read and read and read all day. They send in breakfast and lunch, and you keep reading (and billing). If the company will not let you stay on site after hours, you and your colleagues will go out to dinner and stay overnight in a nice hotel, for which the client pays. If the company does let you stay in their offices, you might be there until 1 or 2 in the morning. Most lawyers find the work tedious, but it's excellent training on how to draft contracts and how to review them for pertinent information. In addition, it's a chance to get to know your colleagues really well. And on rare occasions, you'll get to do a little detective work if the company has not supplied the proper documents and you have to interview employees to determine where they are.

Research and writing memos

Researching legal issues and writing memoranda about them is something that you should learn in law school, as research and memoranda writing are essential for all aspects of a law practice. However, this process is rarely the same in actual legal practice. Not only are memos in corporate law slightly less formal and slightly less constrained by citation rules, your superiors might have very different ideas about what constitutes a useful, readable document. In a corporate law department, you must locate applicable laws and figuring out what practical impact they have on your client's decisions and actions, rather than assessing the state of the law on a certain issue in the abstract. It's important to research and write the memo as quickly and efficiently as possible without sacrificing thoroughness and accuracy. Don't be surprised if your first memorandum comes back to you covered with corrections. And don't let it bother you. Just make sure to incorporate all of the suggestions into your revision and ask questions if you don't understand a comment.

Contract drafting and review

Drafting a contract means preparing the contract from the beginning – usually starting with a form and then tailoring it to fit the needs of the parties. When you write a contract put down in words what the parties have agreed to in principal as best as you can so that there are no ambiguities in the future when the same parties or others read those documents. Then you (or a more senior associate) will go back and forth with the lawyers for the other parties to revise and refine the document until all parties are comfortable signing. Negotiation of the contract involves some compromise. Once you understand what is important to your client and what they can live with or without, you try to strike the best deal for them without risking endless delay or total breakdown of the process. It's best not to spend too much time trying to hash out issues that aren't really essential to your client.

Review of a contract is simply reading the contract to determine what the parties' rights are under its terms and whether any of the terms may be detrimental to your client. When you're starting out, the person who gives you the assignment will tell you what to look for. Ultimately, you will have read so many agreements that you'll know what's standard and what could be disadvantageous to your client.

Formation and "housekeeping" of corporate entities

As a new corporate associate, you will learn to draft basic certificates, like a certificate of incorporation. These certificates are modeled after a form, so such tasks are pretty easy. In many firms, this kind of work is also handled by experienced paralegals, and those paralegals can often be a great source of knowledge for a new associate.

But before you file the papers, someone has to determine what would be the best structure of the organization, depending on the clients' goals. Examples of different legal entities include general partnerships, limited partnerships, limited liability companies, C corporations, S corporations and business trusts. Each structure offers its own legal and tax advantages and disadvantages. For example, a limited liability company, which is a hybrid between a partnership and a corporation, might provide the best tax treatment while retaining the limited liability advantage of a corporation. If the company wants to trade shares on an open market ("go public"), they have to use a standard corporate form, or C corporation, since that is what stock exchanges usually require. For a smaller company, with no immediate plans of going public, an S corporation, which, unlike the C corporation, does not pay income taxes on earnings (instead, the shareholder pays income tax on dividends), might present a better solution.

Forming the company is easy, and a paralegal can usually accomplish this task, although it is a good idea for a new lawyer to learn the process and be able to review the paralegal's work. The hard part is determining what the rights of the owners are in relation to each other, including consideration of how the parties are going to get out of the relationship if they decide their goals are not being met, and making sure that all of this is reflected in the company's documents, whether via a shareholders' agreement or an LLC agreement, in the articles of incorporation or bylaws, or even on the share certificates themselves. As a new lawyer, you won't be making these decisions. Either you'll be executing the instructions of another attorney, or taking a crack at the project yourself and then learning the correct reasoning when the someone else reviews your work.

After you have created a legal entity under the applicable state law, you have to continue to ensure that proper documentation is made of the company's decisions and actions so that there is a clear corporate history of regulatory compliance. Corporate "housekeeping" involves drafting and filing the necessary paperwork to maintain an entity's corporate status with the appropriate governmental entity, usually a state secretary of state's office and the Internal Revenue Service. For example, you may draft or review board of directors' resolutions, file tax records, maintain and prepare stock certificates, and draft partnership or shareholder agreements.

Often, small companies are formed without the advice of a lawyer. When this happens, the corporate formalities, other than the filing of simple articles or certificate of incorporation might be largely ignored. This doesn't usually become a problem for the company until it becomes an acquisition target (meaning someone wants to buy the company) or when the company has expanded and wants either to start raising capital through the sale of shares or to go public. At this point, a lawyer will often have to work with the client to recreate the records that the corporation needs and may even have to amend the articles of incorporation to permit for the issuance of additional and different types of shares. You will have either to know or to research the corporate statutes of the state of the company's organization to make sure that the company is in compliance with the state's requirements.

Preparing filings for state and federal agencies

It's likely that a new associate will prepare filings other than corporate organizational documents. At a minimum, an associate will usually get some exposure to corporate securities filings. When a company wants to start selling shares to people who were not involved in the inception and management of the company, that company must share a great deal of information about itself. The kind of information the company must provide and the format in which the information must be provided depend on the level of financial sophistication of its investors. The Securities and Exchange

Commission (SEC) regulates this process. If your client wants to sell shares to all kinds of investors, they "go public" and are "traded on an open market." If they choose to do this, they will be subject to very strict disclosure requirements. The documents they have to produce are lengthy (usually over a hundred pages) and extremely number-intensive. They must comply with very specific rules and regulations. Most associates will spend some time proofreading these documents and researching applicable laws and regulations.

Overview of an Acquisition Transaction

This overview of an acquisition transaction is based on a series of interviews with Daniel Boockvar, in-house counsel at Weight Watchers International, Inc., and a former associate at Simpson Thacher & Bartlett.

Preliminary negotiations and valuation

Company A wants to acquire Company B. The two CEOs talk about this idea for a while and decide that now is the right time. The first question is how much money will be paid for Company B. Company A comes up with a price they'd be willing to pay, and Company B comes up with a price they'd be willing to take.

How do they come up with these numbers? When thinking about corporate transactions, it's important to see the parallels to smaller transactions that individuals engage in routinely. So let's think about buying and selling a house, something many people have an opportunity to do at least once.

When you sell a house, you usually don't put the house on the market yourself. Why is that? Part of the reason is that it's hard to know how much to sell it for. This is where a real estate broker comes in. A real estate broker can look at how much other properties are selling for and assess the value of your property. Taking these and other factors into account, the broker will help you determine an asking price. In some circumstances, the broker will also introduce you to prospective buyers. In a corporate acquisition, the investment banker is like a broker. An investment banker calculates and assigns value to the deal and then sells it for the company.

In a real estate transaction, you often have a buy-side broker as well. This is even more likely in a corporate acquisition. Buyers need someone to show them what's on the market and investigate the deal. A buy-side broker might work to negotiate the valuation of the company. All this can happen before any lawyers get involved. The brokers talk about the price and may even come to a preliminary agreement, which basically means, "This deal looks good to me, but I need to talk to my lawyers and learn more."

In a corporate transaction, this agreement is often memorialized, either in a term sheet or a letter of intent (LOI), each of which is usually non-binding. Such a document simply sets out the fundamentals of the deal -- at a minimum, what you're buying and how much you will pay for it. A term sheet might be one page of bullet points. A letter agreement is a little more formal and can be a little longer. It is also likely to contain more legalese. In addition to a description of the entity being purchased and the purchase price, a detailed letter of intent might include a no-shop provision (which means the seller agrees not to offer to sell the company to anyone else for a certain amount of time), a non-disclosure agreement (which means you'll keep the deal confidential) and a non-competition agreement (which means that once you've purchased the company, the people whose company you've purchased aren't going to go set up a business that compete with yours.) While the agreement to the deal is non-binding, some of these provisions may be binding.

Due diligence

If you were buying a house, you'd need to do an inspection to see whether the boiler works, and whether the roof will hold among other structural issues. If the house is in much worse condition than you originally thought, such information will cause you to reconsider the amount you offered. For example, if you were willing to spend $300,000 for a house because it has a great pool, and then you find out the pool is not usable, you will no longer be willing to spend the same amount of money, since what was important to you about the house is not what you thought it was. In a corporate transaction, the inspection is called "due diligence." Due diligence has three pieces: financial, operations and legal.

Financial due diligence involves proving the financials – confirming that the financial statements are true and correct. An investment banker and/or a financial officer from the acquiring company examine the balance sheets and profit and loss statements of the company line by line to determine whether the company really has the revenue it claims.

Most of the numbers used for valuation are derived from the financial statements.

Operations due diligence involves looking at how Company B (the acquisition target) runs the business. The person who does operations due diligence is not thinking as much about the current transaction and the valuation of the company. He's thinking about whether Company A can live with the way Company B is currently running things, and, if not, how much it would cost Company A to change these practices once they have acquired Company B. How do they manage customer service in their call center? How do they run their warehouse? How does inventory go in and out? What's their marketing like? Do they use TV or radio or print? How is the Human Resources Department organized? How many employees do they have? How are they paid? Do they have unions? Do they have a 401(k) plan?

In legal due diligence, a junior or mid-level associate examines the legal history of the acquisition target and makes sure there are no legal problems that the company hasn't disclosed. The associate reviews the corporate books, which can be a lengthy and technical process. The downside of this work is that it can be tedious. The upside is that it's a good way to learn about how companies work. After reading the corporate minute books, the associate reads all the commercial contracts and looks for the terms of the contract and any provisions that could affect the transfer of the company and business in the future.

For example, if the business of Company B depends on a deal with Intel, and if the terms of the contract between Intel and Company B can be terminated upon a change of control (like the acquisition of Company B by Company A) that can affect Company A's desire to pay an substandard sum of money for Company B.

After examining the corporate books and the commercial contracts, there are other areas to investigate during legal due diligence. Lawyers will look at whether there is any major litigation in process or even the substantial likelihood of litigation. The corporate lawyers in charge of the transaction may bring a litigator from their firm in to evaluate the litigation issues of the target company. Lawyers will examine the employment issues of the corporation. If the employees are organized in a labor union, lawyers will analyze the company's commitments to the employees as memorialized in a collective bargaining agreement. Specifically, the lawyer may need to determine whether and how Company A can terminate Company B's employees. Buyers usually plan to consolidate their labor force to make their companies as efficient as possible.

Lawyers conducting due diligence may also determine whether Company B has any environmental liabilities. If Company B is a unit of GE that has been operating on the Hudson for 30 years, Company A's lawyers should bring in an environmental lawyer to assess the potential liability for any pollution that may have resulted from this operation. Lawyers will also investigate potential regulatory issues. If Company B is doing business in Mexico, you may have to get a handle on Mexico's licensing structure. For example, if Company B is selling food products, this may require certain permits. Company A needs to consult with a Mexican lawyer to advise on what permits are necessary for this. In addition, this Mexican lawyer should also be consulted as to what kind of company can buy a Mexican company.

A corporate lawyer knows enough about all of these areas of law to know what specialists to bring in, either for purposes of gathering or evaluating the information obtained through due diligence. On smaller deals, outside counsel may be cost prohibitive, so an in-house lawyer will have to do most of this work. On larger deals, the in-house lawyer will hire a law firm to help, but generally tries to control costs by doing as much with in-house lawyers as possible.

At the end of the financial due diligence process, the financial statements have either been proven or disputed. If they have been disputed, the parties may renegotiate the price. At the end of legal due diligence, law firm associates produce a due diligence memo (depending on the circumstance, this can be as long as 30 pages) outlining all their findings. If in-house lawyers have done the due diligence, the findings can be reported verbally or in a brief internal memo of a few pages.

Before due diligence, Company A might only understand the assets it can acquire in the deal. The purpose of due diligence is to also understand all the liabilities that come along with those assets. For example, if Company B is an Italian company, Company A may have to reserve severance benefits of three months' salary for every employee Company A planned to terminate. This could add a million dollars of liability for Company A. That's the kind of thing that lawyers uncover during due diligence that might not occur to business executives prior to legal review.

The contract

The buyer's law firm usually creates the initial draft of an acquisition contract. (Company A is at greater risk, so Company A's lawyers should draft the contract to protect Company A as much as possible.) Lawyers don't write acquisition agreements from scratch. If you're working in a law firm, your colleagues and superiors will recommend acquisition agreements from similar deals and suggest that you use those as your starting point. (If you are in-house, you've probably worked on enough deals to have your own collection.) Then you go through the model agreement and change it to reflect the terms of the current deal as you understand it. Then, once due diligence is all or mostly completed, you incorporate everything you have discovered into the acquisition contract. After due diligence, you "go to contract."

Acquisition agreements – regardless of whether they are stock acquisition agreements or merger agreements or asset purchase agreements – all have the same basic structure: Company A promises to pay X million dollars at Y time. The agreement then sets out representations and warranties (which are basically promises.) The seller represents certain things – e.g., that the company is in good financial condition, in compliance with state and local laws, has no environmental liabilities and has the following litigation pending (basically, all the things that were examined in due diligence.)

An acquisition agreement also contains certain conditions of closing. Company A may include the condition of completing due diligence or obtaining board approval or raising money before purchasing Company B. (This is like having a mortgage contingency when you buy a house.)

The next step is negotiating the acquisition agreement. This can be a two-day, two-week or even two-month process. The due diligence is very legal and the acquisition agreement is very legal, so lawyers are in charge of this stage, though they are still working extensively with the bankers and finance people.

At this point in the deal, the operations specialists are no longer involved. In terms of lawyers, a partner or senior associate is negotiating the acquisition agreement and a junior or mid-level associate is still doing the due diligence and drafting any side agreements like side letters, board resolutions and certificates.. The finance people are still working on valuing the company. If in due diligence the lawyers discover a potential liability the finance people from Company A may tell Company B they will only pay $98 million instead of the $100 million they talked about at the beginning of the process. They may agree to pay the other $2 million in six months once they can see exactly how much a certain piece of litigation will cost them, or once they determine how many employees they'll actually need to pay severance. The acquisition agreement provisions on these matters are drafted by lawyers, but they're drafted in consultation with financial experts. The Company A lawyers have to ask the financial people what representations about the financial statements they should ask Company B to make. Note that the senior lawyers and the financial people are typically the ones talking about this, but the junior associate could be in on the conference call (which could be at 11:00 at night), allowing the junior associate to learn about the big picture. The lawyers negotiate back and forth for anywhere from a weekend to three months. And then they finalize a contract and sign a deal.

Contract to closing

Going to contract is signing a deal. And just like when you buy a house, your contract date is not necessarily your closing date. So there's a period between signing the contract and closing during which Company A continues to do due diligence and resolve a few outstanding conditions to closing. The junior associate prepares formal closing documents like non-competition agreements and licensing agreements, board resolutions and secretary's certificates. If the acquisition is particularly large, these lawyers may also prepare the filings needed to obtain antitrust approval. During this period, the investment bankers and financial officers finish raising the money they need, just as a buyer of a house would go out and get a mortgage, and then the closing happens, which means that final documents are signed and the money flows from one bank account into another. That's the official end of the transaction.

After closing

After closing, the lawyers prepare a closing set of all the transaction documents and take care of inevitable left over issues. If the buyer and seller have no ongoing relationship, the lawyers may just have clean-up issues. But there are often situations in which Company A and Company B do have an ongoing relationship. In the residential real estate paradigm, such a situation would occur if the seller wanted to stay in the house for six months after closing and the buyer agreed to lease the house back to the seller for that period of time. A lawyer might be called in if, say, the seller/lessee damages something in the house. Likewise, Company A and Company B might agree to close at a certain time for tax reasons or other considerations, but also agree to

Company B maintaining control for a certain period of time for other reasons.

Commercial transactions

The difference between a commercial transaction and an acquisition transaction is that an acquisition transaction is a company determinative event, meaning that it determines whether the people running the company being acquired will still be running it after the transaction is complete. In an acquisition, they won't be. In a commercial transaction, neither party is losing its identity, they're just deciding how to deal with each other in the future.

When you buy your house or sell your house, you're going to be living in a different house after that point. In this context, a commercial transaction is choosing to get a DVD player instead of a VCR, or choosing to add a wing to your house. These are events significant to household management, but they don't require you to leave your house. A lawyer's role on a big commercial transaction can be similar to that on a merger or acquisition transaction, because, if you need to build a new warehouse for your business, you still need to conduct due diligence to assure that the business will not go bankrupt while working on your facility. If you draft a supply contract with your vendor, your contract will still have representations and warranties and terms and conditions conditions (the promises we discussed in the description of an acquisition transaction). In a commercial transaction, you are memorializing an ongoing relationship of transactions rather than a one-time transaction.

A Day in the Life of a Junior Associate

Here's a look at a day in the life of a junior corporate associate at a medium-sized firm.

8:30 am: Arrive at the office and proceed directly to an internal training session covering an aspect of the year-end reporting process. This training is part of a six-session series presented by the firm every year to prepare the associates for the upcoming reporting season.

10:00 am: Return to office to pick up file on a private biotechnology client and hurry to a meeting with a senior associate. At the meeting, discuss the list of names and addresses of the client's stockholders (mailing list), which I reviewed the day before in preparation for a

Section 228 Notice of Action Taken mailing. Point out to the senior associate which addresses are missing and ask her to obtain these from the client. She also suggests where to look for additional information regarding stockholder addresses.

10:30 am: Discuss the upcoming Section 228 Notice of Action Taken with my assistant. This particular mailing will be to nearly one hundred stockholders. You have found that if you discuss upcoming large projects with your assistant in advance, she is more likely to clear her schedule of other work and help you complete the project in a timely manner.

10:35 am: Take a few minutes to check e-mails from the night before. Most of them discuss various due diligence issues that have been uncovered during document review for a merger. (I am working on a team with a mid-level associate and a partner on a merger of our client with and into another biotechnology company.)

10:50 am: Briefly review estimated corporate tax forms from California that need to be forwarded to another client. Draft a cover letter to the client to accompany the tax forms and instructions.

11:15 am: Meet with the mid-level associate to discuss various merger diligence issues and the "to-do" list for the day.

11:30 am: Proofread the cover letter to be sent with the tax forms and instructions and send the packet to the client.

11:40 am: At the request of the mid-level associate, call opposing counsel to discuss a new diligence question. Take notes of discussion. Copy a few documents from the master diligence file for the review of the mid-level associate and bring the copies to her office.

12:10 p.m.: Eat lunch in office. Organize e-mails from the previous day while eating. Moving e-mails from the Inbox into client-related folders helps you to locate relevant messages quickly.

1:00 p.m.: Revise the mailing list for the Section 228 mailing to incorporate new information provided by the senior associate. Find additional information in a closing binder that the senior associate provided during the morning meeting. Check the mailing list against the stock ledgers to ensure that all stockholders are accounted for. Give the list to assistant so that she can get an early start on preparing mailing labels.

2:15 p.m.: Prepare a first draft of Disclosure Schedule to the Agreement and Plan of Merger. Briefly meet with the mid-level associate to give her a copy of the draft and to share thoughts about further improvement of the draft.

6:00 p.m.: When I return to the office, I find an unexpected voice mail from a public company client regarding the latest edits to an Amendment to Form S-2, which the client plans to file with the SEC the next day. I have been involved with the drafting of the Form S-2, but not with this particular round of edits, which were made by a senior associate. Call the client back and discuss the edits with her, pointing out that she should further discuss a few of the edits with the senior associates the next morning.

6:20 p.m.: Prepare and send a long e-mail to the controller of the client involved in a merger asking him to provide some additional information for inclusion in the disclosure schedule and to help with the preparation of a few sections of the schedule.

6:50 p.m.: Receive and review e-mail from opposing counsel containing additional questions in connection with her due diligence review of our client's documents.

7:00 p.m.: Call opposing counsel to discuss her due diligence questions. Answer two questions, and promise to follow up on the others and call her back the next day with the answers.

7:15 p.m.: Forward the unanswered due diligence questions to the mid-level associate for her review.

7:20 p.m.: Revise the draft disclosure schedule to incorporate the comments made by the mid-level associate during our last meeting. Leave a copy of the revised schedule in her office for her review.

8:00 p.m.: Organize files and prepare a tentative "to-do" list for the next day.

8:15 p.m.: Leave the office and hurry to catch an 8:30 train home.

Another Day in the Life of a Junior Corporate Associate

As discussed earlier, your working life is very dependent on the specific firm and city in which you practice. The economy also plays a role, as is clear from the following lawyer's diary. Here we take a look at a day in the life of a second-year Minneapolis corporate associate during the 2001-2002 recession.

5:45 a.m.: Wake up, walk dogs.

6:15 a.m.: Read *U.S. News & World Report*, *Pioneer Press* news and sports sections.

6:50 a.m.: Shower, have breakfast.

7:20 a.m.: Play with dogs.

7:40 a.m.: Drive to work with wife.

8:05 a.m.: Check voice mail and e-mail; one new voice mail message from client regarding their credit facility.

8:15 a.m.: Read Star-Tribune.com and American Lawyer online.

8:35 a.m.: Meet with partner regarding the credit facility which is to be signed today.

9:10 a.m.: Draft legal opinion for bank client regarding hedge funds.

10:00 a.m.: Receive call from client regarding a merger and the shareholder meeting to approve the merger which is two days away.

10:35 a.m.: Draft script for shareholder meeting.

11:15 a.m.: Telephone call with an acquaintance regarding a potential new securities litigation matter.

11:45 a.m.: Meet with senior litigation partner to discuss whether we can represent the parties in this securities litigation matter – it appears unlikely.

12:30 a.m.: Lunch with four other corporate associates in an adjacent food court.

1:25 p.m.: Research and draft the legal opinion regarding hedge funds. I came across some sticky points which is quite frustrating.

3:45 p.m.: Meet with partner to discuss our firm's legal opinion for the credit facility. We walk through the back-up that I have put together for the opinion. We are still missing a signature from the written action of the client's board approving the credit facility terms and we can not issue the opinion until this is received.

4:25 p.m.: Receive call from Canadian client to discuss the credit facility. The client will not be able to get the signature on the written action until tomorrow morning so we will not sign up the credit facility until then.

4:45 p.m.: Draft legal opinion for bank client regarding hedge funds.

5:00 p.m.: I am to go to dinner and a basketball game tonight with a client. Research this client on the Internet and review names and backgrounds of the people that will join us for dinner and the game so we can discuss current things occurring at the client's business.

5:15 p.m.: Meet with three partners in the lobby and walk over to restaurant.

5:30 p.m.: Dinner with clients at Italian restaurant.

7:00 p.m.: Attend basketball game with client using the firm's tickets (second row - courtside).

9:35 p.m.: Game ends; say goodbye to client and walk to car.

10:20 p.m.: Walk dogs, talk with wife about plans for this weekend; call friend to arrange social engagement on Saturday.

10:45 p.m.: Receive call to attend a benefit auction on Friday evening.

10:50 p.m.: Go to bed.

Words of Wisdom for the New Associate

The most frequently offered advice for junior associates is twofold: first, ask questions, and second, listen carefully. Make sure you ask enough questions that you understand both the assignment and the format in which your response is expected – while some senior associates or partners might want a 50-page memo, others are expecting a simple oral report. One second-year associate stresses the importance of getting as much as possible from each assignment, urging lawyers to "put in the time to go the extra mile to learn what you are doing." There is so much to learn, so many documents you've never seen before, that the sooner you can pull yourself over this learning curve, the better off you'll be.

The other area of practice frequently addressed by experienced attorneys is lifestyle adjustment. One associate in Dechert's corporate securities group advises new lawyers to prepare themselves mentally for the erratic worklife of a corporate associate. In the first few years of practice, he says, there is "no typical schedule." You will have "many days when you are doing almost nothing from 9 till 4, and then the phone suddenly rings at 5:00 and you stay in the office all night." While one lawyer agrees that one of biggest challenges for a young lawyer is learning how to handle the lifestyle, she believes that each new associate should determine what works with her personal schedule and then put her foot down to impose some control. It is important, she emphasizes, to take an early and assertive approach to designing your career path. While clients undoubtedly "would love you to be at the office at all hours," you can, and should, set boundaries.

Mid-level Associates

After a few years, an associate will start supervising more junior associates in researching and writing memos, filing basic corporate documents and due diligence reviews. A mid-level associate will have a larger role in transactions. You become responsible for drafting key contracts for a deal and for taking and processing people's comments on them. This usually involves taking a merger document from a deal that has been completed, and altering it based on information you get from a partner about how this deal is different. You prepare a first draft and give it to the partner to review. The partner sends it back to you with comments and suggestions. The partner may then ask you to show the document to a tax lawyer, an employee benefits lawyer or a real estate lawyer for comments. You'll make changes to the document until everyone in your firm is happy with it. Then you or your partner will send it off to the other party's lawyers. Depending on how complicated the deal is, you might get to negotiate whether to use these changes or leave the document as is. Otherwise, your partner or senior associate will handle the negotiation, returning the suggested changes or compromise language to you so you can implement them.

At some point, you may also be responsible for creating a transaction checklist, a list of all the documents that need to be drafted, reviewed and signed before the deal is complete. You may be asked to file disclosure information about parties to an acquisition or merger with the Department of Justice and the Federal Trade Commission.

As you gain seniority, you should be able to draft and negotiate more complex contracts, such as stock purchase agreements and complex merger agreements, firm opinions and shareholder agreements. You should also be able to form limited liability companies and draft securities filings. In addition, you will become more comfortable with advising a client who may be trying to decide how to structure an acquisition or a joint venture.

Sometimes, chance dictates the progress of your law firm career. "When I was a second year," says a lawyer with seven years of experience, "I was very fortunate because we were short-staffed, so I was assigned to several large M&A deals, one of which was an auction. All of the associates were sending out forms to all of the bidding companies and doing their markups while our company was deciding which company they wanted to do the deal with. This meant that I got a whole lot of experience and training working with a senior associate, which in turn meant that a partner gave me one to do on my own when I was a second-year. When I handled that transaction well on my own, I was given a leasing transaction to evaluate on my own, and then a document to review and negotiate and revise on my own."

In general, the more seniority you achieve, the more often you will negotiate documents with opposing counsel, have responsibility for documents and oversee deals. This means that you will have more opportunities to give a client advice and manage your client's expectations and supervise (and train) more junior associates. Just how much more direct client contact you will have after your second or third year depends on the nature and size of the client. Larger, more institutional or long-time clients tend to deal with partners, while smaller clients might work with associates, both because of partners' higher billing rates and because associates are generally more accessible. It also depends on how busy a firm is – in a very busy firm, client contact can come much earlier in an associate's career.

(See the Appendix for model corporate documents.)

A Day in the Life of a Mid-level Corporate Associate

Take a peek at a day in the life of a mid-level corporate associate at a medium-sized firm.

8:30 a.m.: Arrive at the office and read the local business journal or business section of the newspaper. (Local companies still make up the bulk of most firms' business.) Skim through any trade publications looking for articles relevant to clients' industry sectors. Note any articles that might be interesting to send to clients.

9:00 a.m.: Start responding to e-mail and voice mail messages from the night before. E-mail will contain requests for contract drafting or review and/or questions about documents you have previously drafted. Spend time creating the day's to-do list, noting where input from more senior attorneys is needed and where matters can be delegated to more junior attorneys.

9:30 a.m.: Long conference call with opposing counsel to discuss the comments which you circulated yesterday on the asset purchase agreement and related documents opposing counsel had drafted. You explain point by point why the changes are necessary for your client, and you and the opposing counsel negotiate the agreements. Business issues that require input from the clients are tabled – i.e., purchase price adjustment, other changes in economics.

10:45 a.m.: Just off your conference call, you check your messages: two are from senior attorneys in the firm. One senior attorney wants to give you his comments on venture documents you drafted last night. Another wants you to participate in a client pitch at 4 p.m. The third message is from a public company client that has a securities law question. You haven't talked to this client in three weeks, but the client calls you for periodic legal advice.

10:45 a.m.: Call back the public company client first. The client asks you whether certain company information needs to be filed with the Securities and Exchange Commission immediately or whether it can wait until the company's next quarterly filing. You tell the client you'll look into it and get back to them today.

10:50 a.m.: Stop by the senior attorney's office who left you a message about the venture documents. He tells you his thoughts and comments on the documents. This is another matter unrelated to the asset purchase agreement you were negotiating in the morning. Most corporate attorneys handle several deals at once. You explain to your assistant which of his comments to incorporate into the documents and leave the assistant to make the changes.

11:00 a.m.: Call back the other senior attorney. He asks you to participate in a client pitch later that day at 4:00. You are asked to pull some forms of agreements the firm uses for its biotech clients.

11:10 a.m.: Call the client regarding the asset purchase agreement you were negotiating in the morning. Summarize the tone and contents of your call with opposing counsel and ask for the client's feedback on the business issues that were tabled. Take notes.

11:15 a.m.: Research the securities law question that was raised from your public company client. Call a senior attorney to confirm the results of your research.

11:40 a.m.: E-mail the company that is awaiting the venture documents to let them know they will be coming this afternoon and that you are just incorporating the senior attorney's comments. Frequent status updates are an important part of client relations.

11:45 a.m.: Call back the public company client and explain the information must be filed as soon as possible with the SEC and tell them you will prepare the filing. Enlist the help of a junior associate to prepare the filing.

11:55 a.m.: Call the opposing counsel back on the asset purchase agreement and explain your client's business position and comments.

12:15 p.m.: Go to lunch training session. Most large firms have periodic training sessions on relevant corporate law topics.

1:15 p.m.: Pull together a package of form agreements for the client pitch this afternoon.

1:30 p.m.: Proof the changes to the venture documents which were entered by your assistant. Read through the documents in their entirety looking for any last minute changes. Make last minute changes. Distribute the documents to your client with a long cover memorandum explaining what each document contains.

2:00 p.m.: A client you periodically field calls from asks you to draft a compensation package for a new Chief Scientific Officer who will be relocating to the area for this job. You begin drafting the offer letter, employment agreement, option agreement, etc.

3:15 p.m.: The junior associate sends you a draft of the SEC report for the public company client. You interrupt your drafting of the compensation package to review it and get comments back to the junior associate.

3:40 p.m.: Resume drafting the compensation package.

4:00 p.m.: Meet the senior attorney in a conference room for the client pitch. The two of you explain deals you have done in the recent past and why your firm will serve this client better than all of the other firms in town. Listen to the client present its business.

5:00 p.m.: Finish drafting the compensation package and get it to the senior attorney for review before it goes out to the client. Call the client to say you will have it to the client by tomorrow afternoon.

5:30 p.m.: The junior associate sends you the revised SEC filing for the public company client. You review, add comments and then distribute to the client.

5:45 p.m.: A client calls you unexpectedly to discuss a term sheet the client just received from a venture firm in California. You walk the client through the terms of the deal and explain how you think the terms vary from the current market terms. The client asks you to mark up the term sheet with your comments.

6:15 p.m.: You review and mark up the term sheet based on your client's needs as just discussed. You send a blackline of the term sheet to your client for further review.

7:00 p.m.: On a particularly busy day, 7 p.m. is the best time to start drafting agreements as clients and senior attorneys generally aren't calling anymore. Before going home, you check with opposing counsel to see if she plans to distribute revised versions of the asset purchase agreement and related documents tonight or tomorrow. As the documents will come tomorrow, you can go home. If they were coming tonight, you would likely stay another hour to review the revised agreements (depending on the timing of the deal)

Moving to a Smaller Firm

Once you have worked in a large law firm for a few years and you want to move elsewhere, you have some choices. You can go to another large or medium-sized firm for more money, slightly different work or a new set of colleagues. You can also move to a smaller law firm. At a large firm most of your work will consist of drafting documents for senior associates or partners. Since large law firms tend to have large institutional clients, those clients, the CEOs, the COOs and CFOs, like to deal with partners or with senior associates. This means that a junior associate will have very little interaction with the clients themselves. A move to a small firm can mean much more significant contact with clients earlier on in a career. Since small firm clients, for the most part, are smaller entities themselves, lawyers at all levels of experience have more opportunities to build relationships with officers of start-up companies and other institutions and to advise them in a broad scope of law and business.

One lawyer from a small in-house department of a corporation sees another advantage of working with a smaller entity. "There seems to be a lot more congeniality in our small group than I ever felt in law firm corporate departments or even in my experience at the larger in-house legal department of my previous corporate employer. I think that working with people who have impeccable ethics and who care about the welfare of their employees can make a big difference in your happiness as a lawyer. I personally feel that one is more likely to find such people in smaller firms and smaller legal departments. This is not to say that lawyers in large firms are unethical. However, large firms have large overhead costs and therefore tend to be more focused on the bottom line than on the training and happiness of their associates."

The Life

CHAPTER 8

Handling Assignments

The most important thing you can do to advance your legal career is to pay attention to detail. Don't cite cases you haven't "shepardized." (Attorneys use Shepard's Citations to track case history, including whether a decision has been overruled, modified or qualified by more recent opinions.) Don't drop zeros in your transaction documents. No one will care how innovative or creative or smart you are, or even how many hours you are working, if you make mistakes in your work. Business people can afford to glance over a document before signing it because they rely on their lawyers to study that document before it gets to them. You have to be determined to survive in a service-oriented environment. Be a careful lawyer who goes the extra mile.

With partners and other associates, the best way to get along in a law firm is to do your best. If you do make mistakes and you become discouraged, don't give up and start decreasing your effort at work! If you're taking the time to do your best and pay attention to detail, you will get more support and have better work relationships.

Using technology

Most office environments have been changed by new technologies. Things are no different in the law. If you're a very well-established senior partner, you may never touch a computer, but that's only because you have a smart, well-trained secretary to interface between you and the rest of the firm. A junior associate will absolutely have to use technology to get work done and communicate with the rest of the office. If you have never worked in an office before, you may have to get used to simple technologies like a multi-line phone system, fax machines, copiers and sometimes even scanners. If you're in a small firm, you may not have enough support staff around to help with these things. If you're in a larger firm, the support staff might be around, but they might be following the orders of more senior lawyers, leaving you to negotiate your own relationship with each piece of equipment, and to suffer the consequences if that equipment fails to do what you ask of it.

A working computer, printer and software are critical to corporate lawyers, especially in a smaller law firm setting where you enjoy little support and you must be autonomous in getting your documents prepared and distributed to the relevant parties. The ability to use technology also aids in legal research and drafting. E-mail and the Internet are incredibly useful tools for research and transfer of documents. Lawyers can do entire closings by e-mail, which can save a great deal of time and paper. Technology also allows lawyers to do more things remotely -- from home, from a client's office or even from an opposing counsel's office.

In the past, many firms gave each new associate a daily planner and encouraged associates to plan their time carefully (and bill their time even more carefully). Today, some firms have gone so far as to give associates BlackBerries or other handheld PDAs, which means that associates can always be reached by e-mail. This can be frustrating when you just don't want to be reachable for a few hours, but it also means you can check your messages and, if there's nothing urgent for you to do, go to the office a little later occasionally.

Billing Your Time

Most clients pay for the time lawyers spend working on their behalf. (In some cases, though less frequently in corporate practice, fees are based on a contingency and lawyers take a percentage of the verdict or value of a successful transaction, rather than charge an hourly rate.) Clients, therefore, demand a strict accounting of what each lawyer (and paralegal) is doing during each segment of time for which they are compensating the firm. Thus the billable hour system was born. Most clients require that lawyers keep track of their time in either tenths of an hour or quarters of an hour. If you are billing for tenths of an hour, this means you must account for your billable time in six-minute increments. For example, a 12-minute conversation with a client might be recorded as "Phone conference with client A about the status of the indemnification negotiations on the Purchase and Sale Agreement – 0.2 hrs.

To associates' dismay, much of their working time is not billable. Marketing, internal firm meetings and retreats, lawyer recruiting, general research projects for client development purposes and administrative work are not billable. Some clients will not allow lawyers to bill their travel time. That means it takes considerably more time to bill eight hours than eight hours. Excluding lunch, which is of course non-billable, an associate can expect that at least one hour of each working day will be non-billable. And that's on a good day, with ample billable work. On a "bad" billing day, you might spend all the hours between 9 and 4 working on a non-billable research project you've been putting off. When 4:00 rolls around and a partner drops a billable project in your lap, you might be frustrated because you feel you must stay late to get that project done so you don't get behind in your hours.

Some lawyers don't mind the billable system at all, saying that marking your time on each client matter and reporting it on a daily basis becomes second nature. They also point out that the billing record acts as a measure of their productivity each day and forces them to manage their time better. However, just as many lawyers claim that billing by the hour encourages inefficiency and takes an extraordinary amount of time.

What is a Billable Hour Requirement and What Does it Mean to Your Life?

Okay, so you keep track of what you do all day. What's the big deal? Well, for many people the big deal is the billable hour requirement. Firms don't just expect you to keep track of your time; many expect their associates, and their partners, to work and bill a certain minimum number of hours each year. Sometimes meeting this requirement determines whether you receive a salary increase or a year-end bonus. In a large firm, this number, which is sometimes presented as a requirement, and sometimes as a goal, is usually between 1,900 and 2,100 billable hours per year. Many associates work substantially more than that.

These numbers might not mean much to you now, but once you begin to practice, they will become an important part of your life. For example, 2,000 hours translates into 167 hours per month or about 39 hours per week, 52 weeks per year. If you add another several hours each week for non-billable matters and assume that you might take at least a couple of weeks of vacation, it becomes increasingly clear that you'll spend some very long working days and/or weekends to meet your firm's billable hour expectations.

"It is very hard to strike a healthy balance between your work and your personal life," says one associate. "You are lucky if you can manage to get one or two weeks of vacation and a handful of holidays." Even though the firm may observe a holiday, like the Fourth of July, you still must account for those hours, which means either working later the rest of the week or working on Saturday or Sunday. Many lawyers say that the pressure to bill more hours in order to move up in a firm can lead to abuse of the system – for example, associates reporting two hours spent on a project when they only spent one hour.

At the top firms in the country, meaning the ones with the biggest clients and the highest salaries, the requirement can sometimes be as high as 2,500. One corporate lawyer suggests that 3,000 is a more accurate figure. There are rumors that these firms keep cots on hand for their highest-billing associates. On the other hand, other big firm associates suggest that while there are certainly attorneys who work more hours, 2,000 hours are "fairly doable." Those who move to smaller or medium-sized firms in smaller cities might find a different work schedule. Sometimes there's no talk at all of the billable hour requirement. These associates are encouraged to use their vacation days and estimate that they bill around 1,500 hours. Many lawyers currently working as in-house counsel cite the billable hour requirement as the single most important factor in their decision to leave private practice.

The Ebb and Flow of Transactional Work

One aspect of a corporate attorney's life that new lawyers might find hard to adjust to is the absence of a regular schedule. There really is no typical day for corporate lawyers. This ebb and flow is perhaps unique to transactional practice, with some days so slow and devoid of work that associates surf the 'Web all day, and others subject to such tight time constraints that lawyers work straight through several nights to complete a deal. One veteran attorney suggests that this unpredictability has both benefits and drawbacks. On the other hand, it is difficult for associates to plan ahead. On the other hand, there is no time clock to punch and many lawyers can take advantage of downtime to leave early or work from home.

"I don't think someone who hasn't practiced in a large firm can understand the totally demanding nature of what we do," explains one mid-level associate. "Not only are we on call 24/7 for whenever that all-night project comes in, we are often asked to juggle competing demands. If you're not adept at prioritizing and organizing, you can't do this job. If you need predictability, you can't be a corporate lawyer. You have to be extremely dynamic and able to roll with whatever happens. You have to like frantic work periods followed by relatively slow periods of rest."

Compensation

So what's the reward for all this work and the demanding hours? It's the elephant in the room during every job interview -- the money. Many law firms like to keep these numbers secret, both from the outside world and from their employees. However, the law firms that form NALP (the National Association for Law Placement) have agreed to share information about entry-level salaries, and you can often find salary figures for top firms in other sources, such as the *Vault Guide to the Top 100 Law Firms* or "The NLJ 250," *The National Law Journal's* annual survey of the nation's largest law firms.

After the first year, the rates at which salaries increase are firm-specific. Each year of associate experience brings several thousand dollars in increased compensation. Raises almost always depend on reviews of the associate given by senior associates and partners. By the time you're an eighth-year associate, you could be making anywhere from $90,000 in a small firm to $180,000 in the largest firms. Geography also plays a big role. Associates in New York, Chicago, Los Angeles, San Francisco and Washington, D.C., have higher salaries than associates in cities like Detroit and Fort Lauderdale. Most firms don't offer the same pay in their satellite offices across the country. This means that you could be working for the satellite office of a New York firm, working "New York hours" and making a regional salary, which might be nearly half of what your Big Apple colleagues make in the same year. Of course, the cost of living in your area will also likely be substantially lower than that of New York.

Some firms have two compensation tracks based on the number of hours an associate bills. They might let you opt for a 1,700- or 1,800-hour track and pay you a lower salary than that given to associates who work a higher number of billable hours. Other firms give everyone at the same level who meets a certain minimum number of hours a "lockstep" salary increase. Those firms reward higher hours and client development with year-end bonuses. Some of these firms make all bonuses discretionary, and others make them automatic for associates who meet certain billing levels. Bonuses often range between $5,000 and $15,000.

Between raises and bonuses, it's not unrealistic that an associate's salary could double within three years. But in the current, weaker market, the forecast is less rosy. This does not necessarily mean that an associate's salary will be cut. Large firms tend to lay off attorneys before they touch the salaries of those attorneys they choose to keep around. The layoff trend follows the larger economic cycle. In down times, it's harder for weaker candidates to get and keep jobs. In a really strong economy, a law firm might have so much work that it would keep on a weaker associate just to get the work done, even knowing that the associate wouldn't advance to senior associate or partner status.

Golden handcuffs

In corporate law, more than any other type of legal practice, a well-credentialed new associate will start making a great deal of money right away, likely much more than that person has ever made before. John DeRosa believes that a good law school career office should counsel law students about what this is going to be like and how this money will affect their lives three years into their law career. He refers to this as the "golden handcuff" syndrome. "New lawyers are working really hard for this money, so they build their lifestyle around it and might be spending just as much as they bring home," notes DeRosa. "If those lawyers find they don't like their jobs or want shorter hours or a different kind of work environment, they feel trapped by the kind of money they're used to spending." DeRosa advises that new lawyers build a budget based on a salary of $50,000 a year, even if they make $125,000. He explains that by using all the excess to pay down school debt, many lawyers can pay off their loans after three years and then have the freedom to take an in-house job or move to a smaller firm if they want such a change.

While budgeting for a change in circumstances is a smart idea, one experienced associate offers a word of caution about viewing experience at a big firm merely as a launching pad to a career elsewhere. Francesca Lavin discourages new lawyers from looking at big-firm corporate practice simply as a way to spend a couple of years to earn some money and get basic transactional experience. A large firm, she notes, is like any other place of employment; it might be daunting at times, but it might also be a satisfying place to spend a good part of your career. Go somewhere they feel comfortable and to plan to stay as long as they remain comfortable. And keep in mind that more and more firms are willing to accommodate attorneys who want reduced or flexible schedules and alternatives to the partnership track.

Location and Size of Firms

If you go to a national law school, especially one on the East Coast, you'll probably find an emphasis on getting a job at a large New York law firm. A New York firm can be the ultimate pedigree after a national law school. The salaries are tremendous and the prestige and training will follow you for the rest of your career. But there is a trade-off. "If you want a fast-paced business environment, there's no better place to practice law," says one New York lawyer. "If you don't like a fast-paced environment, it's not going to be good for you – you're going to work long hours and there's going to be a lot of pressure and stress. But if you handle stress well, the rewards are great and New York is the place to be."

There are other advantages to working in a large firm. The resources are fantastic. You meet and work with new people all the time. If there is a partner you want to ignore, you can probably avoid that person and still get plenty of work elsewhere. In addition, you have more people whose opinions you can seek when you have a tough new issue to address. Larger firms typically provide more secretarial support, more word processing and more paralegals, in addition to a dedicated business development staff.

Some lawyers find a medium-sized firm in a smaller city to be a good compromise. "You can't do the most sophisticated work that New York firms do, but you won't be working 2,500 hours a year either," says a Boston associate at a 500-attorney firm. "It's a good mix of challenging work and decent lifestyle." A Minneapolis lawyer agrees. "The trade-off is a more reasonable hourly requirement and a lower cost of living in exchange for a much lower salary. A medium-sized firm like ours, with around 400 lawyers, is large enough to attract significant-sized businesses as clients. Such clients generate good legal work and are able to pay for it – that makes transactional practice more comfortable, although somewhat less hands-on. The partner-associate ratio isn't out of whack, which means an associate is doing more interesting work and is closer to the client than he or she would be in one of the truly large firms."

Work and Family Issues

Being a lawyer in a firm is not an easy first job to have. If you decide to add a family to the mix, you have some hard decisions to make. If have taken on debt, you might want to stay with the highest-paying job you can get so you can repay your debts and earn the experience you will need to progress in your career. As we see in the day in the life of a corporate partner, some parents do successfully practice full-time in a law firm. Others want more time outside work to spend with their families. Some firms have responded to this desire with part-time and flexible hours options for partners and associates.

"Part-time" and "flexible hours"

These policies depend on the firm. Given the typically long hours a full-time corporate lawyer works, a "part-time" schedule might be 1,600 billable hours, which could mean working 9 to 5, Monday through Friday. Most firms have flexible hours; they don't care when you work, so long as you get the work done and keep your clients happy. Many firms tailor these options to specific lawyers. Some people can work seven days a week, but need to work from home on some days. Other lawyers have several days a week during which they do not work at all. Usually, the hours actually worked are matched to a percentage of compensation comparable to their reduced deal load or caseload. Associates report that in addition to having a percentage of compensation deducted, working part-time can also detrimentally affect bonuses, raises and chances of making partner.

"We have a number of women who work 80 percent time and it seems to work for most of them," reports a large-firm associate. However, the attorney adds, "you have to have a certain kind of personality to walk out the door and not come in on your day off. Clients and other lawyers in the firm will never understand which day you take off and will leave you messages on that day. You [must] have a strong personality to insist on only working 80 percent time and you have to be damn good as well, otherwise clients will prefer someone who is always available. People will respect your schedule but only if you insist upon that respect. It's not for those who are easily guilted into things."

Other associates have observed different trends. "Law firms have a long way to go toward making [part-time schedules] viable options for practicing law," says an attorney who recently moved from a large firm to an in-house position. “I don’t know of anyone who has made a part-time practice in a firm large work.”

One associate notes that many firms have responded to attorneys’ desire to balance work and family life by adopting policies that allow reduced schedules for associates and partners as well as alternatives to the partnership track, such as counsel or senior attorney. She urges associates to speak up and to work out an arrangement with their firm rather than to bow out early, leaving in anticipation of difficulties. “You’d be amazed,” she says, how willing many places are to accomodate you if you are a good lawyer, and if you tell them what you want.

Moving Up and On: Partnership and Lateral Moves

CHAPTER 9

After several years as an associate, with accompanying increases in levels of salary and responsibility, you and your firm will have to decide what's next for your career. Many associates dream of becoming partners at their firms, having sole responsibility for client relationships, sharing decisions about the future of the business as a whole and benefiting from the financial rewards of corporate America. At large firms, it takes between seven and 12 years to make partner. Typically, you'll have an idea of whether you're on track for partnership (meaning you bill sufficient hours and bring in enough clients) by your fifth or sixth year.

If you're not in the running, or don't want to be a partner, then you might have the option of staying on as special counsel or of counsel. This position means different things depending on the firm. At some law firms, an attorney with this title is simply a (highly) salaried employee too senior to be considered an associate. At others, or in other circumstances, of counsel are given a percentage of the money earned from work they bring in. This compensation scheme is less common, because if the attorneys were bringing in a great deal of work, they would probably have been offered a partnership position.

Perhaps a greater blow than realizing you're not going to make partner is NOT realizing you're not going to make partner. Only a few of those associates competing for partnership will actually share in the wealth and prestige of the position. This means that many associates work very hard for 10 years or so, only to find themselves passed over for partnership year after year. (In the meantime, of course, they are making high salaries, getting bonuses and acquiring useful contacts and tremendous experience.)

Making Partner

What happens when you become a partner, achieving that title you have pursued year after year? Life may not immediately change. You may have a higher level of responsibility, but in order to make partner you've already been taking on more and more responsibility as a senior associate. You've trained associates and managed associates and had more direct contact with clients. While as an associate the main source of pressure in your life was the quest to become a partner, your new challenges are to develop business and to integrate work within the firm.

Lawyers can generate business in many different ways. They can distribute marketing materials, give speeches and participate in trade organizations. Another method is to develop relationships with other partners and opposing counsel. If a litigator has a client who needs to rethink corporate structure, he can put in a good word for a corporate partner whom he respects. Internal referrals can be one of the largest sources of new business for a partner. Opposing counsel might refer clients as well.

In the past, at some firms there was a division between rainmakers (the partners who brought in the work) and the partners who did the work. Today, there are only a few firms, usually those with institutional clients, where a lawyer can be a partner without generating business. Most firms rely on every single partner to bring in business.

A Day in the Life of a Corporate Partner

This day in the life is a snapshot of the life of a relatively young New York corporate partner who is also the mother of a young child.

Note that outside New York, partners at top firms work a similar number of hours, but they tend to work them earlier in the day. One partner at the Washington, D.C., office of Arent Fox, for example, gets in the office around 7:45 a.m. and stays until 7:30 p.m., usually five days a week, with an occasional weekend. These partners report that their schedules do not generally decrease as they advance at a large firm, because the pressure to bill and record time to measure production doesn't go away.

6:15 a.m.: Wake up.

6:30 a.m.: 40 minutes on StairMaster with *The Wall Street Journal* and Walkman; read front page, op-ed pages and "Money & Investing."

7:10 a.m.: Play with toddler daughter – read books, play with toys, watch dogs, buses and taxi cabs from window.

7:30 a.m.: Make coffee and daughter's breakfast; drink coffee.

8:00 a.m.: Play with daughter.

8:30 a.m.: Nanny arrives. Discuss day and play with nanny and daughter.

8:45 a.m.: Check voice mail and e-mail; four new voice mail messages including voice mail from colleague regarding transaction for Client A -- Client A wants to accelerate closing for end of month (two weeks away!) – Propose call at 4:00 p.m. on revised documents; get ready for work.

8:55 a.m.: Drink more coffee; get ready for work.

9:30 a.m.: Cab to office with newspaper; call assistant – No new messages. Call associate re: transaction for Client A and get update on status; associate believes new proposed closing date is very aggressive particularly in light of annoying opposing counsel.

10:00 a.m.: Arrive at office; check voice mail and e-mail; receive call from Client B regarding an agreement that needs to be drafted relating to a deal that was recently closed; Client B needs letter agreement by following day.

10:15 a.m.: Call from Client C regarding new deal -- wants to invest $25 million in company with publicly traded debt -- Client C has worked with lead investor on transaction and wants to review, provide comments and sign off on documents by end of day; discuss transaction with Client C.

10:45 a.m.: Conduct conflicts search with respect to new target company for Client C.

10:50 a.m.: Receive call from associate regarding questions related to preparation of organizational documents for a start-up company (Client D); refer associate to examples of charter and bylaws we have prepared for similar clients and we discuss some of the key points in the documents and making sure that the start-up company will have the flexibility it needs.

11:00 a.m.: Review draft of investment agreement for Client C.

1:15 p.m.: Contact senior and mid-level associates to staff transaction for Client C; brief associates on background, timing and key points of deal.

1:30 p.m.: Order lunch and eat at desk while continuing to review investment agreement.

1:45 p.m.: Receive call from Client C; discuss significant deal points on new transaction with Client C.

2:30 p.m.: Conduct internet research on potential new client in preparation for a lunch meeting with a potential new client the following day. Contact business development department to request relevant materials and press articles on our firm's practice and recent transactions.

2:45 p.m.: Meeting with associates regarding investment document related to new transaction for Client C.

3:00 p.m.: Begin to review revised equity documents (shareholders agreement, stock purchase agreement, registration rights agreement, charter and bylaws) regarding transaction for Client A in preparation for 4:00 call.

4:00 p.m.: Receive call from opposing counsel on matter for Client A. 4:00 p.m. call has been pushed to 5:00 (thankfully).

4:10 p.m.: Client D (start-up company) calls with two of its founders. They have several questions on corporate governance issues and matters that need to be addressed in organizational documents. I propose call for following day at 10:30 a.m.

4:15 p.m.: E-mail associate working with me on organizational documents for Client D to confirm her availability for 10:30 a.m. call.

4:16 p.m.: Continue to review documents on matter for Client A in preparation for 5:00 call.

4:45 p.m.: Call from Client B regarding changes in required letter agreement. Client needs revised letter by 7:00 p.m.

4:50 p.m.: Call associate on matter for Client B to confirm that associate is drafting agreement and discuss points raised by client. Continue reviewing documents for Client A.

5:10 p.m.: Meet with associate working on matter for Client A and discuss revised documents.

5:15 p.m.: Conference call begins with opposing counsel on matter for Client A; discuss remaining open points in stockholders agreement, stock purchase agreement, registration rights agreement, charter and bylaws. Develop list of open points to be discussed with our respective clients.

6:25 p.m.: Call ends. Associate and I call Client A to discuss open points in equity documents.

6:30 p.m.: Client C calls (and interrupts call with Client A). He would like me to join him in a meeting with the lead investor and lead investor's counsel on new matter. Meeting to begin at 7:00 p.m. Client would like us to first address the significant business issues with the lead investor and opposing counsel, then both clients will leave and he hopes that I can continue to work through the legal and contract drafting points with opposing counsel. The goal is to have a document ready to sign by later in the evening or the following day.

6:33 p.m.: Rejoin call with Client A; summarize significant open points based on 5:00 p.m. call and propose 9:30 a.m. call the following morning to review all open issues.

6:40 p.m.: Call senior associate on matter for Client C regarding impending meeting.

6:45 p.m.: Review draft letter agreement for Client B.

7:00 p.m.: Prepare for meeting and leave office with colleague to go to opposing counsel's office on matter for Client C.

7:05 p.m.: Meeting with client, lead investor and lead investor's counsel. Discuss and resolve several of the significant business issues.

8:30 p.m.: Client C leaves. My colleague and I continue to negotiate with lead investor's counsel regarding the remaining business and legal issues in the document. Together we develop a list of open business issues for our respective clients.

9:50 p.m.: Client C calls the conference room. He is transferred to another conference room where my colleague and I discuss the remaining open issues with Client C. I advise him of their proposals and suggest counter proposals. We discuss risks and benefits of deal and typical provisions for comparable transactions.

10:10 p.m.: We rejoin the main conference room with counsel for lead investor. The lead investor returns and Client C calls in. We discuss open points and resolve significant open points. Certain points will continue to be discussed following revised draft. Lead investor's counsel will revise document and circulate document overnight. We agree to review document and call opposing counsel midday after discussing revised document with Client C.

10:30 p.m.: Car home. Check voice mail. Five messages including two calls from junior associates on matter for Client C. I call associate and update him on the meeting. We discuss various issues in the meeting that will need to be confirmed in our due diligence.

10:45 p.m.: Arrive home. Check e-mail. Send responses to e-mail messages.

11:15 p.m.: Go to bed.

Compensation

Partner compensation varies from firm to firm, and it's hard to get specific information on numbers. At most firms, compensation is determined by a similar formula, which includes overall financial compensation, number of hours billed and number of clients developed. If you take responsibility for or service clients another lawyer has brought into the firm, this will be factored in as well. (Some firms call this an attribution, and some a working attorney credit.)

Your Ongoing Job Search

It's the rare lawyer who stays with the same firm for the whole of his career. In fact, a recent NALP survey reported that 60 percent of large firm associates changed jobs at least once in the first five years of practice. Lawyers move for a change of hours, compensation or firm resources. If you are not interested in staying on at your firm because you don't think you'll make partner or don't want to make partner there, you have several options. You can move to a different firm. You can go in-house to one of your clients. Some lawyers with backgrounds in finance may join an international organization that engages in large transactions.

The lateral interview

Interviews are different when you're being considered for a lateral hire than when you are starting out as a lawyer. The attorneys who interview you expect you to know exactly what you want. They expect you to have significant experience in the area of law you practice, and they expect you to be able to articulate that experience in an enthusiastic and knowledgeable way. And, in order to hire you, the interviewers will have to be convinced that you'll fit into the firm environment and that you are committed to staying with the firm for a long time. "In lateral hiring, most people are looking for someone who practices in a way that's similar to the way they practice," reports Rich Gale, a partner in the D.C. office of Arent Fox. "When a client asks a partner for advice, some partners will want their associate to provide an answer in a 20- to 30-page memo and others just want a quick answer in a phone call."

When you move from one law firm job to another, you are coming from a position of strength. So, it's a good idea to spend time researching the firms with which you interview to determine whether they will really be a good fit for you and your career goals. This is another area for which informational interviews are indispensable. The recruiting partner at the firm is not going to tell you whether the corporate partner who needs an associate is pleasant to work for and whether he has power in the firm. But lawyers do talk about their firms with other lawyers. If you're hooked into the legal community, or know people who are, you can avoid getting yourself into a work situation that will be detrimental to your career. You can instead seek out colleagues and superiors who will make your career pleasant and satisfying.

Legal recruiters

Looking for legal employment can be a very time-consuming process. Law firm partners and, at larger firms, in-house recruiters receive a tremendous number of resumes. They save themselves time and effort by establishing relationships with specific executive (attorney) recruiters to help facilitate faster, higher quality placements. The firms know which independent recruiters can effectively screen job applicants and learn to trust them to provide good candidates for interviews. This allows the law firm recruiters to take care of entry-level and summer clerk hiring and the partners to focus on the business of the firm.

Working with independent recruiters also offers an advantage for job-seeking attorneys – anonymity. Don't jeopardize your current job with rumors that you're looking for work. A legal recruiter can take your resume and show it to firms on an anonymous, or at least confidential, basis.

When working with a legal recruiter, a candidate generally provides a resume, writing sample and transcript to the recruiter, who will interview the lawyer over the phone or in person. The recruiter checks the education, licenses and references of the candidate. The recruiter either markets the candidate's resume to a firm or presents the resume to a law firm in response a request from the firm. The recruiter helps to schedule interviews with the firm, to negotiate the terms of an offer and to facilitate offer/counteroffer matters.

Your law school career office

You undoubtably used your law school career office to get a job the first time around. Depending on the school you attended, you may still be able to use this office as a resource for a lateral move. Most offices offer job listings in some form or another such as print newsletters or password-protected web sites. Many of these listings come from other alumni who know of job openings elsewhere or who have openings in the entities where they work. Most career planning offices also offer some counseling for graduates, perhaps a one-time phone session to strategize about a job search. A few offices have a full time alumni career services counselor on staff, whose only job is to assist alums with their career moves. If your alma mater has someone like this on staff, you should use this invaluable resource.

Last, but certainly not least, is that invaluable network of friends, colleagues and alumni that you used as a first-time job seeker. This can be even more helpful to you as a practicing attorney.

Beyond the Law Firm

CHAPTER 10

Working In-house

Perhaps you've heard lawyers and law students liken their search for an in-house position to a quest for the Holy Grail. What's so different about this kind of position? What do these lawyers do?

"Running a business is all about establishing relationships to help your business run," explains Daniel Bookvar. In-house lawyers structure, document and solidify the relationships for your organization. These lawyers create contracts with suppliers, and contracts with customers, and contracts with the people who keep the lights on. These are commercial transactions. The most technical transactions are usually outsourced. If you think of your relationship with your doctors, the in-house counsel is like the general practitioner. He's the one with the close relationship with the patient, and he knows how the arm relates to the head and how the head relates to the neck bone, but he's not the guy you pull in for hand surgery.

The duties of an in-house attorney can vary greatly depending on the company and the position. Some lawyers with corporate law training end up managing litigation in addition to drafting and negotiating contracts and leases. "I get in between 9:00 and 9:30 and leave between 7:00 and 7:30," reports the in-house counsel of a New York media company. "As soon as I get in there's a phone call from a business person asking me to look at a document or asking me to help out with something. I'm constantly looking at documents, marking them up and having discussions with the business people about how long we want the term of sale to be, or how to establish pricing, or 'Gee, does this really make sense given what you've told me?' I'm constantly on the phone, either with my own clients (the company's business or sales people) or with the other side. It's an incredibly interesting day."

For many attorneys, their jobs in the legal departments of corporations end up involving more than pure legal work. They also use an intuitive or acquired understanding of the business side of the company. It's often at in-house positions that an MBA or equivalent business training will prove most helpful.

The advantages of going in-house are many. Some in-house lawyers set their own hours and can choose to work at home on occasion, while others must follow stricter schedules and be in the office between certain hours of the day. Many lawyers, particularly in smaller legal departments, feel a greater sense of autonomy than they did as associates at a law firm. Since the company has hand picked them from large law firms, the company assumes these lawyers are already well-trained and do not need to have their work constantly reviewed. This independence can be a tremendous change for an attorney coming out of a large firm. Some have described it as feeling as though they're "finally back in control" of their lives.

Many lawyers also thrive on the constant communication with the business people of the country. Every lawyer cites the freedom from billable hours. "The billable hour requirement," muses one in-house attorney, "just makes things worse. I think I've worked more hours straight through while in-house than while I was in a law firm. I think the pressure to constantly be billing hours in some ways slowed me down. Now I don't even think about it; I just get a lot of work done because I have a lot of different things that have to be done."

Another difference between practicing in a firm and working in-house is in the type of agreements in-house lawyers draft and negotiate. Companies aren't usually buying and selling each other every day, so in-house lawyers no longer do as much of the merger and acquisition work common among large law firm associates. Instead, they focus on what the company does on a daily basis, which could be selling a product or a service or pieces of real estate. In-house lawyers report that this work involves very different agreements and takes place at a completely different pace. Commercial law (the law of buying and selling goods and services) uses a more standard form contract and many of the discussions are around purely commercial terms – such as the pricing, the quantity, and so on.

A Day in the Life of an In-house Corporate Media Counsel

7:00 a.m.: Wake up.

7:30 a.m.: Spend 45 minutes at the gym.

8:15 a.m.: Shower, dress, eat breakfast, watch SportsCenter

9:00 a.m.: Leave for work.

9:20 a.m.: Arrive at work. Check voice mail and e-mail.

9:30 a.m.: Return phone calls; catch up with colleagues.

9:45 a.m.: Respond to e-mails that can be answered in a few lines or less.

10:30 a.m.: Attend meeting of attorneys in my division. Discuss any substantive legal questions the attorneys may have regarding issues arising during contract negotiations.

12:00 p.m.: Grab lunch.

12:30 p.m.: Check voice mail and e-mail.

12:45 p.m.: Return phone calls and respond to e-mails that can be answered in a few lines or less.

1:45 p.m.: Begin reviewing client comments on license agreement and preparing revised agreement.

3:00 p.m.: Have emergency, unscheduled conference call to finalize license agreement.

5:00 p.m.: Meeting with business people regarding idea for new sale. Show up at meeting late because unscheduled call ran over.

5:30 p.m.: Check voice mails and e-mails.

5:45 p.m.: Return phone calls and respond to e-mails that can be answered in a few lines or less.

6:30 p.m.: Continue to revise license agreement.

7:00 p.m.: Send revised license agreement to client. Review a licensing agreement from a vendor.

7:30 p.m.: Leave for tomorrow morning the process of typing into the document my hand-marked comments to the license agreement. Go home.

Working for the Government

Another option for lawyers interested in corporate matters is to work for a government agency. Corporate lawyers can work for a number of different agencies in the government. At the federal level, they work for the Securities and Exchange Commission (SEC), the Federal Trade Commission (FTC), the Commodity Futures Trading Commission (CFTC), the Federal Reserve, the Federal Deposit Insurance Corporation (FDIC), the Federal Communications Commission (FCC), the Justice Department and the Central Intelligence Agency, among other places. (If you want to know what sort of work corporate lawyers do for the CIA, check out the CIA Office of General Counsel web site at http://www.cia.gov/ogc/best.htm.) Lawyers can also find jobs related to corporate law in state and local government. For purposes of this book, federal jobs will be the focus, because they tend to provide the most transferable experience to the private sector.

How much do government lawyers make?

Each government agency has its own salary rate for attorneys, and each attorney will be offered a different starting salary depending on credentials and experience. Most entry-level attorneys are hired at the GS-11 or GS-12 pay rate. The United States Office of Personnel Management (OPM) posts federal employee pay tables every year on the OPM web site (www.opm.gov). For 2003, GS-11 attorneys might be paid between $42,976 and $55,873, while the range for GS-12 attorneys is between $51,508 and $66,961.

The SEC web site lists the following salary ranges for attorneys in the Washington, D.C., metropolitan area:

- One year of legal experience: $72,000 to $92,000
- Two years of legal experience: $86,000 to $110,000
- Senior/supervisory positions: $99,000 to $153,000

"There is a great disparity in pay between government lawyers and private-sector lawyers," says one lawyer who has worked for the government since 1989. "How much of a disparity depends a lot on where you live. If you're out in the middle of nowhere, government jobs can be fairly price-competitive. There are cost of living adjustments, but they don't make up for the difference in cost of living. I make $98,000 a year. If I were living in Iowa, this would be a great salary, but D.C. is getting more and more expensive. If I were to go to a private sector job now, even if it were in a boutique firm rather than a large firm, I would be paid between $125,000 and $200,000. The conventional wisdom is that there is a trade-off, since the hours of a government lawyer are so much better than those of a big firm job. But this isn't always necessarily true. When I worked at the U.S. Attorney's office, we worked 80 hours a week."

How can you get hired?

There are three ways to get hired as a federal government lawyer. The first is to go through a hiring program sponsored by an agency. Several agencies have honors programs for entry-level lawyers and internships for law students. The second method is to reply to a job listing. Government job listings can be found in the same places as other legal job listings, and also in The National and Federal Legal Employment Report. (See www.attorneyjobs.com for information on how to obtain a paid subscription.) The third way (you guessed it!) is through networking. Attorney jobs in the federal government are coveted. Just because they must be advertised doesn't mean that hiring is done on a completely objective basis. Of course, an internship is the best way to network. If you've interned with an agency and made a good impression, it will be a lot easier to get a permanent position with that agency.

Pros and cons of working for the government

The number one advantage of a government legal job is the fact that you can have work hours that are close to a 9-to-5 job. You can also have a flexible work schedule; some lawyers have every other Monday off, others have job share situations with other attorneys. "No one expects you to miss a friend's wedding or a doctor's appointment," explains one SEC attorney. "As a government lawyer, my clients are the investors of the United States. I'm not usually dealing with them. Instead, I'm dealing with the corporations who want to issue stock to them. So there's less pressure to drop everything to make the corporation happy. I can weigh the relative importance of a particular phone call or critique of a document versus the other work on my plate and my other life obligations. Some agency staff attorneys have never worked a weekend or stayed past 5:30 on a weekday. Others might work 7 a.m. to 12 a.m. for a month, then take a week off without asking for permission. The trade-off is that we make a lot less money."

A government job sometimes offers more interesting work than an entry-level job in the private sector. If you're in the right agency at the right time, you will do cutting-edge work, rather than document review. A government lawyer might have lots of high-level contact at the very beginning of his career. "Usually, an SEC staff attorney will be the sole contact on a major deal within the first month of the job," says one SEC lawyer. "If you're not comfortable with responsibility right out of law school, this might not be the right job for you." Government jobs also provide good benefits and a comfortable retirement. In addition, your work serves the American people in a way other corporate law jobs will not.

There are tradeoffs for these advantages. As noted above, the most obvious disadvantage of working for the government is the compensation. "What's most disturbing to me is that, relative to other employees in this agency, your law degree doesn't mean anything," says one government lawyer. "You could be a high school graduate and be making almost the same salary I make now. If you come out of law school with a ton of debt, your federal government job will not help you pay it down. However, this kind of job would qualify you for loan forgiveness, if your law school has a hefty enough endowment to offer it." Moreover, some government agencies won't pay for bar dues, continuing legal education or other perks typically provided by a law firm.

Other tradeoffs are less immediate. "Many government lawyers fear that they will become so specialized that they will no longer be able to get a job outside the government," reports one government attorney. "The flip side is that there are certain places in the government that will give you experience in your first year that you won't get for the first seven or eight years of your law firm job, and there are some niches in the government that have incredible marketability on the outside. If you choose to work for the government, just make sure that you learn a marketable skill set, whether you want to stay in the government for the rest of your career or not."

Working at the SEC

The Securities and Exchange Commission is one of the more obvious choices for a career as a corporate lawyer in the public sector. Lawyers at the SEC are advocates for investors. Every time a corporation wants to go public, these lawyers study the documents the corporations distribute to investors and their financial advisors and make sure that enough information is clearly stated so that investors can make a rational decision about their money. The SEC is organized into four divisions: Corporation Finance, Market Regulation, Investment Management and Enforcement.

As a staff attorney, most of your time is split between your phone and your computer. You draft and issue comment letters, which critique the offering materials companies supply to you. You write no-action letters to those companies and internal memos describing your decisions. Once a week, you attend commission meetings. Every time new rules are adopted, you print them out and study them so you will be prepared to answer questions that come in. "The connections you can make here are amazing," raves one SEC attorney. "I know senior partners and corporation executives all over the country. I think that when I move to the private sector, I'll have a better shot at being a partner, because I already have a reputation for competence with the decision-makers."

There is a potential drawback for those hoping to change direction after starting their careers at the agency. A corporate attorney working for the government might not get much training or experience in basic lawyerly skills such as negotiating and drafting. One SEC lawyer with several years of experience plans to move to a law firm to obtain this experience and training and open up her career options. "I've had offers to go in-house," she says, "but I don't think it would be a good idea to take them without law firm experience." Moreover, moving up in the SEC takes a long time, and many lawyers move back into law firms before transitioning to the private sector. "Even if you want to move higher up in the government or work for a broker-dealer," she says, "law firm training is important."

How can you know if a job at the SEC is right for you?

"Before taking a job at the SEC, you should think about how well you do in terms of telephone interaction versus face-to-face interaction," suggests an SEC veteran. "My work involves phone consultations and documentation of those phone consultations," she says. "In four years, I've had two in-person meetings." A job at the SEC is also extremely accounting-intensive. "You have to read and evaluate financial statements from the very beginning," says the SEC staff attorney. "It's really smart to have a working knowledge of accounting before you get here. Our formal training program is weak: we hear lectures once a week for four months. These lectures are so broad, it's difficult to apply the information to anything you're working on." Not that private-sector lawyers necessarily know their accounting principles any better. "Law firm associates don't know how to spot accounting issues," she reports. "They miss them all the time."

On a day-to-day basis, your colleagues in a government agency can be very friendly and are probably less cut-throat than those at a large law firm. But, as with any job situation, there are politics to assess and certain codes of behavior to follow. At a law firm you might be able to avoid a partner you don't get along with. At the SEC, the staff attorney notes, "here there's a clear hierarchy. Your superior is your superior, and your colleagues are your colleagues. There's a high premium placed on getting along with other people. You have to make sure everyone likes you if you want to advance. In a law firm, people will tolerate a talented, hard-working jerk. At the SEC," says the staff lawyer, "such a person won't get fired, but he won't advance either. If you're coming in as a lateral, be careful not to insult the lawyers who started their careers in government. Those lawyers haven't done the transactions they are regulating. Many of them have an inferiority complex about it."

Day in the Life of an SEC Staff Attorney When No Commission Meeting is Scheduled

9:00 a.m.: Arrive at office, read The Wall Street Journal for relevant articles related to the Commission, check voice mail and e-mail.

9:30 a.m.: Begin returning phone calls.

10:00 a.m.: On days when the Commission does not meet, review registration statements that have been filed and amendments to registration statements. Screen out registration statements to receive reviews from the staff. Return telephone calls to attorneys. Answer interpretive questions relating to the Securities Act of 1933 and Securities Exchange Act of 1934. Meet with staff accountants to discuss overlapping accounting and legal issues involved with ongoing registration statement reviews. When necessary, consult with other divisions (Investment Management, Market Regulation, Enforcement) to address issues arising out of registration statements. When necessary, consult with Corporation Finance support offices (Office of Chief Counsel, Office of Mergers and Acquisitions, Office of International Corporation Finance) to address specialized corporation finance issues arising from registration statements. Discuss status of filings and issues with outside counsel.

12:00 p.m.: Lunch/attend staff training session.

1:00 p.m.: Review registration statements that have been filed and amendments to registration statements. Screen out registration statements to receive reviews from the staff. Return telephone calls to attorneys. Answer interpretive questions relating to the Securities Act of 1933 and Securities Exchange Act of 1934. Meet with staff accountants to discuss overlapping accounting and legal issues involved with ongoing registration statement reviews. When necessary, consult with other divisions (Investment Management, Market Regulation,

Enforcement) to address issues arising out of registration statements. When necessary, consult with Corporation Finance support offices (Office of Chief Counsel, Office of Mergers and Acquisitions, Office of International Corporation Finance) to address specialized corporation finance issues arising from registration statements. Discuss status of filings and issues with outside counsel.

5:30 p.m.: Leave work.

Day in the Life of an SEC Staff Attorney When a Commission Meeting is Scheduled

9:00 a.m.: Arrive at office, read The Wall Street Journal for relevant articles related to the Commission, check voice mail and e-mail.

9:30 a.m.: Begin returning phone calls.

10:00 a.m.: Attend Open/Closed Commission meeting. These are meetings where the five members of the Commission meet to discuss and approved proposed and final rules, enforcement actions, and other issues of importance to the Commission.

12:00 p.m.: Lunch.

1:00 p.m.: On days when the Commission has adopted proposed rules or final rules, go to SEC web site (www.sec.gov) and print off the adopted proposed/final rule, if available. Read rule and familiarize with substance of the new rule and implementation timeframe for new rule. Print out press releases regarding these rules and study them as well.

5:30 p.m.: Leave work.

Temping as a Lawyer

"Temporary employment for attorneys has become more and more popular for a multitude of reasons," reports Terri Williams, regional vice-president for Special Counsel, Inc. "It allows attorneys more flexibility with their schedules. They can work during certain periods of time and choose not to work during other periods of time. Temporary attorneys frequently comment that they have made the move to temporary work because of quality of life considerations, not having to concern themselves with billable hour requirements.

Temping as an attorney is a good way to get to know firms and to determine where one wants to work on a direct hire basis. And in some cases, it provides a candidate with an opportunity to get their foot in the door, allowing the firm to get a good look at the candidate and vice-versa. Finally, it is a great way for an attorney to get experience in a practice area in which they may eventually wish to practice on a regular basis."

The pay rates for temporary lawyers vary based on the expertise and experience required by the client as well as the type of client. Clients are increasingly attuned to the bill rates charged by staffing companies for contract lawyers. The pay rates range from a minimum of $20/hour for document review to well over $100/hour for more substantive work. "Temporary legal work is a great opportunity for those who graduate from law school without a job offer," says Scott Krowitz, a partner in the temporary placement firm Lexolutions. "The work gives young lawyers exposure to the practice of law and creates new networking opportunities. And temp-to-perm (temporary to permanent) positions can lead to permanent jobs that might not have been available to these attorneys through the usual recruiting channels."

APPENDIX

Appendix

Note on appendix materials: Do not rely on the legal analysis, content, case law or structure of any of the following model documents and memoranda. They are provided only to increase your understanding of what corporate lawyers do and the kind of documents with which they work. All of the identifying information and much of the information necessary for the documents and memos to be complete has been redacted.

- **Writing Sample**
- **Sample Memoranda**
- **Sample Corporate Documents**
  - Service Contract
  - Promissory Note
  - Opinion Letter
  - Limited Liability Company Operating Agreement

Writing Sample - Courtesy Nellie Kate Estes, Student at Florida Coastal School of Law

MEMORANDUM
MUCK, EDDY & MUCK
BALTIMORE, MARYLAND

To: **Professor Scales**
From: **SGN**
Re: **Trade Secret issue**
Date: **December 26, 2002**

Facts: Our client, Shock Cola, Inc., would like to know if its cola recipe will be considered a trade secret in a misappropriation claim against Mild Cola, which has obtained the Shock Cola recipe. Buddy Blaha, Mike McCormick and George Edwards spent two years researching and developing the recipe for Shock Cola. The recipe took very little money to develop; however, it would take two years of effort for another company to properly acquire the recipe by trial and error. Except for the three who developed it, only Mr. McCormick's girlfriend knows the recipe and she was sworn to secrecy.

Although Mr. McCormick and Mr. Edwards still own equal shares of the company, Mr. Blaha manages the company on his own. Mr. Blaha keeps the Shock Cola recipe in the top right-hand drawer of his desk. He had kept the recipe in a locked box until a week before the incident. He has written the word "confidential" across the top of the page that contains the recipe. His desk does not have a lock, and Mr. Blaha rarely locks his office door.

Mr. Blaha hired an executive assistant to help organize his office. There was a stack of papers on his desk, and Mr. Blaha asked the assistant to take them to a copying service. Earlier in the day, Mr. Blaha had been looking at the recipe, when an emergency caused him to drop the recipe on his desk and leave the office. He did not realize that the recipe was among the papers that the assistant took to be copied.

The employee at the copying service noticed the paper that contained the recipe and kept a copy of it. He then sold it to Mild Cola, one of Shock Cola's competitors. Mild Cola will not be able to increase its revenues by selling cola made with the Shock Cola recipe, but if it sold the cola at very low prices, Mild Cola would increase its market share and would drastically harm Shock Cola's revenues.

<u>Question Presented:</u> Under section 11-1201(e) of the Maryland Commercial Law Code, is Shock Cola's recipe a trade secret where two years of research were expended in developing the recipe; few persons knew of the recipe; the only copy was kept in a drawer in the company manager's desk; a competitor would have to research for two years to duplicate the recipe; and, because of the recipe, the company's revenues were twenty million dollars a year?

<u>Short Answer:</u> Probably yes. Shock Cola's recipe is probably a trade secret under the Maryland Commercial Law Code, because few people know the recipe; reasonable measures have been taken to guard its secrecy; it is of substantial value to Shock Cola and its competitors; great effort went into developing it; and great effort would have to be undertaken for others to duplicate it.

<u>Applicable Statutes:</u>

Md. Com. Law Code Ann. § 11-1201(e). Maryland Uniform Trade Secrets Act; definition of Trade Secret.

"Trade secret" means information, including a formula,pattern, compilation, program, device, method, technique,or process, that:

(1) Derives independent economic value, actual or potential, from not being generally known to, and not being readily ascertainable by proper means by, other persons who can obtain economic value from its disclosure or use; and

(2) Is the subject of efforts that are reasonable under the circumstances to maintain its secrecy.

<u>Discussion:</u> Before adopting the Uniform Trade Secrets Act in 1989, Maryland courts used the Restatement of Torts' six factor test in determining whether information is a trade secret. The factors are: (1) the extent to which the information is known outside of the business; (2) the extent to which it is known to employees and others in the business; (3) the extent of measures taken to guard the secrecy of the information; (4) the value of the information to the business and its competitors; (5) the amount of effort or money expended in developing the information; (6) the ease or difficulty with which the information could be properly acquired or duplicated by others. See Restatement, Torts, § 757 b.

The definition of a trade secret contained in the Maryland Uniform Trade Secrets Act (MUTSA) is based on this section of the Restatement. See Optic Graphics, Inc v. Agee, 87 Md. App. 770, 784, 591 A.2d 578, 585 (Ct. Spec. App. 1991). Although MUTSA preempts the Restatement, Maryland courts continue to apply the Restatement's six-point test as helpful guidance in determining the existence of a trade secret. Home Paramount Pest Control Cos. v. FMC Corp./Agric. Prods. Group, 107 F. Supp. 2d 684, 692 (D. Md. 2000). Therefore, the six-point test will be applied in this case to determine whether there is a trade secret as set forth under MUTSA.

In addition, there is little case law in Maryland concerning trade secrets. To determine if there was a trade secret in this case, it is helpful to discuss the holdings from courts in other states. The out-of-state cases cited below also use the Uniform Trade Secrets Act, as well as the six factors laid out in the Restatement in determining a trade secret.

The recipe in the present case conforms to the first part of MUTSA because it is considered a formula. The Restatement's six-part test is applied to the instant case as follows:

1. The extent to which the information is known outside of the business.

The court will probably find that Shock Cola satisfied this element because only one person outside of the business knew of the recipe, and that person was sworn to secrecy.

Limited knowledge of a trade secret by a few persons outside of the business will not necessarily negate the trade secret status. See Space Aero Prods. Co. v. R. E. Darling Co., 238 Md. 93, 112, 208 A.2d 74, 83 (1965). In Space Aero, the court held that although the company's silicon manufacturer knew of the trade secret and tours of the facility were conducted, this knowledge did not negate the secret status of the information. Id. However, the information can not be public knowledge. See Enterprise Leasing Co. of Phoenix v. Ehmke, 197 Ariz. 144, 149, 3 P.3d 1064, 1069 (Ct. App. 1999). In Enterprise, the court held that a trade secret may not be available in trade journals, reference books, or public materials known to trade persons who can gain benefit. Id. However, a trade secret may consist of a combination of elements even though individual elements may be a matter of public knowledge. Coca-Cola Bottling Co. of Shreveport, Inc. v. Coca-Cola Co., 107 F.R.D. 288, 289 (D. Del 1985). In Coca-Cola, the court held that the Coke recipe was a trade secret even though the individual ingredients were common knowledge. Id. In addition, the owner of a trade secret may, without losing protection, disclose it to a third party, if the disclosure is made in confidence. See, Kewanee Oil Co. v. Bicron Corp., 416 U.S. 470, 475 (1974).

In the instant case, the recipe was not public knowledge, and the only person outside the business to know the recipe was Mr. McCormick's girlfriend. The court will likely find that Mr. McCormick's disclosure to his girlfriend will not destroy the recipe's status as a trade secret, because he told the recipe to her in confidence. Mild Cola may argue that because the ingredients in Shock Cola are public knowledge, there is no trade secret. However, like the Coke recipe in Coca-Cola Bottling, the secret to Shock Cola's recipe is its combination of ingredients. Therefore, the court will probably find that these facts satisfy this element of the test.

2. The extent to which it is known by employees and others involved in the business.

In the instant case, no other employees know the recipe for Shock Cola; therefore, the court will probably find that this element is satisfied.

3. The extent of measures taken to guard the secrecy of the information.

The court will likely find that Shock Cola took reasonable measures under the circumstances to guard the secrecy of its recipe, thereby satisfying this element.

Absolute secrecy is not essential, but a substantial element of secrecy must exist to keep others from properly acquiring the information. Space Aero Prods. Co., 238 Md. at 109, 208 A.2d at 82; see also, Tabs Assoc., Inc. v. Brohawn, 59 Md. App. 330, 347, 475 A.2d 1203, 1212 (Ct. Spec. App. 1984). In Space Aero, the company kept the blueprints of its trade secret in a lock box, to which only authorized personnel had access. 238 Md. at 111, 208 A.2d at 83. The court held that the actions taken by the company to protect the trade secret were sufficient to meet the basic criterion of success. Id. at 112, 208 A.2d at 83. Similarly, in Tabs, the operations manual that contained the trade secret was marked "trade secret" and locked in the supervisor's desk drawer. 59 Md. App. at 345, 475 A.2d at 1211. Here, the court held that the company had taken adequate measures to protect its trade secret. Id. at 348, 475 A.2d at 1213. Also, the court in Space Aero held that the fact that no other company had been able to duplicate the information was evidence that the company had taken reasonable measures to protect its trade secrets. 238 Md. at 112, 208 A.2d at 84.

In addition, the court in Enterprise held that the measures taken to protect the secrecy of a trade secret need not be extreme or expensive, but must be reasonable under the circumstances. 197 Ariz. at 150, 3 P.3d at 1070 (holding that the company made reasonable efforts to maintain the secrecy of the information by having a confidentiality provision in its employment agreement). Several courts have also held that the accidental disclosure of a trade secret does not negate its trade secret status. See Fireworks Spectacular, Inc. v. Premier Pyrotechnics, Inc., 107 F. Supp. 2d 1307, 1310 (D. Kan. 2000); B.C. Ziegler & Co. v. Ehren, 141 Wis. 2d 19, 26, 414 N.W.2d 48, 52 (Ct. App. 1987). In Fireworks, the office manager inadvertently mailed the company's trade secret to eleven customers. 107 F. Supp. 2d at 1308. The court held that the trade secret status survived this accidental disclosure. Id. at 1310. Similarly, in B.C. Ziegler, where a company accidentally sent portions of its customer information to a scrap paper dealer, the court found that this did not negate the fact that the company took reasonable steps in protecting the secrecy of the trade secret. 141 Wis. 2d at 26, 414 N.W.2d at 52.

In the present case, the steps taken by the manager of Shock Cola to protect the secrecy of the recipe were similar to those taken by the managers in Space Aero and Tabs. In Space Aero, the documents were kept in a locked box. Similarly, Mr. Blaha kept the Shock Cola recipe in a locked box up until a week before the incident. After that, the recipe was kept in his desk, as were the documents in Tabs. Mild Cola will likely argue that Mr. Blaha's desk was not locked, nor was his office, and that keeping the recipe there did not constitute proper steps to guard its secrecy. However, Mr. Blaha was the only one with access to the locked box and his desk, and keeping the recipe there constituted reasonable measures under the circumstances. In addition, because no other company had previously been able to gain access to the recipe, the court will probably find that reasonable measures were taken to protect its secrecy.

Mild Cola could also argue that because Mr. Blaha left the recipe on his desk, and it was accidentally disclosed to the copying service, he failed to take reasonable measures to protect its secrecy. However, this incident is similar to the one in Fireworks, in which the manager accidentally mailed the company's trade secret to several customers. Because Mr. Blaha had previously taken steps to protect the secrecy of the recipe, and his failure to place the recipe back into his desk was caused by an emergency, the court will likely find that Shock Cola did take reasonable measures under the circumstances to guard the secrecy of the recipe.

4. The value of the information to the business and its competitors.

The court will probably find that Shock Cola satisfied this element because the recipe was of great value to Shock Cola as well as its competitors. Courts have used various methods in determining whether information is of value to a business and its competitors. In Tabs, the court found that the trade secret was the essence of the business and was the sole reason for its profitability and was, therefore, of great value to Tabs and its competitors. 59 Md. App. at 345, 475 A.2d at 1211. Additionally, the court in Space Aero found that the trade secret was of value to the business because the company had grown from a small business into a five million dollar a year business after the new method of making hoses was implemented. 238 Md. at 110, 208 A.2d at 82. In the Coca Cola case, the court held that the recipe for Coke was of great value because the disclosure of the recipe would be extremely damaging to Coca Cola's business. 107 F.R.D. at 294.

In contrast, the court in Optic Graphics, Inc. v. Agee, 87 Md. App. 770, 785, 591 A.2d 578, 586 (Ct. Spec. App. 1991), held that the company's market strategy and pricing information, while valuable to Optic Graphics, was not of value to its competitor because it involved too many variables that were subject to change. Similarly, in Home Paramount, the court found that this element was not satisfied because the business's list of customer addresses and phone numbers was of little value to Home Paramount's competitors. 107 F. Supp. 2d at 693.

In the instant case, the Shock Cola recipe, like the trade secret in Tabs, is the essence of Shock Cola's business. In contrast with Space Aero's growth of five million dollars per year, Shock Cola has enjoyed a much larger amount of growth. It has grown into a twenty million dollar a year business. In addition, as in the use of Coca-Cola's recipe, the use of Shock Cola's recipe by its competitor would drastically harm Shock Cola's revenues. Mild Cola may argue that because using the recipe would not increase its revenues, it is of no value to Mild Cola. Although Mild Cola would not be able to increase its revenues by using the Shock Cola recipe, it would be able to increase its market share, and might even be able to put Shock Cola out of business. The mere fact that Mild Cola is planning to use the recipe would give credence to the assumption that it is of value to Mild Cola, otherwise, it would not use the recipe. Therefore, the court will probably find that the cola recipe is of value to Shock Cola as well as to its competitors.

5. The amount of effort or money expended in developing the information.

The court will likely find that this element is satisfied because it took Shock Cola's owners two years of full-time research to develop the recipe.

A substantial amount of effort or money must be expended in developing the information. In Space Aero, the research that led to the development of its trade secret method of making hoses began in 1950. In 1953, the hoses were sold to several companies. Therefore, the research took no more than three years to complete. 238 Md. at 102, 208 A.2d at 77. The court found that this method took years of experimentation and research, as well as a quarter of a million dollars to develop. Id. at 110, 208 A.2d at 82. Likewise, in Bond v. Polycycle, Inc., 127 Md. App 365, 374, 732 A.2d 970, 974 (Ct. Spec. App. 1999), the court found that the two years of research and $500,000 put into the development of the trade secret was substantial enough to satisfy this element.

In the instant case, Mr. Blaha, Mr. McCormick, and Mr. Edwards put in two years of full-time research to come up with the recipe for Shock Cola. This is similar to the developers in Space Aero and Bond, who took 2-3 years to develop their trade secrets. Mild Cola could argue, however, that because the developers of the Shock Cola recipe did not expend very much money, this element of the Restatement is not satisfied. However, the element only requires that effort or money be expended. Therefore, since the recipe did take substantial effort to create, the court will probably find that this element has been satisfied.

6. The ease or difficulty with which the information could be properly acquired or duplicated by others.

The court will probably find that Shock Cola satisfied this element because the recipe was never duplicated before, and a competitor would have to expend substantial time and effort to duplicate it.

Several courts have held that information can be considered difficult to duplicate merely by the fact that competitors have failed to duplicate it. See Space Aero, 238 Md. at 122, 208 A.2d at 84; Tabs Assoc., Inc. 59 Md. App. at 346, 475 A.2d at 1212; Optic Graphics, Inc., 87 Md. App. at 785, 591 A.2d at 586. In addition, the court in Tabs held that the process could have been duplicated only with properly acquired information by the expenditure of considerable time, effort and money on research and experimentation. 59 Md. App. at 346, 475 A.2d at 1212.

In the present case, as in Space Aero, Tabs, and Optic, Shock Cola's recipe has never been duplicated before. It would also take another company two years of research to duplicate the recipe. Like the trade secret in Tabs, a competitor would have to expend considerable time and effort to duplicate Shock Cola's recipe. Thus, the court would probably find that because Shock Cola's recipe has never been duplicated before, and it would take considerable effort for another company to duplicate it, this part of the Restatement is satisfied.

<u>**Conclusion:**</u> In conclusion, the court will probably find that the Shock Cola recipe is a trade secret under the definition of MUTSA. Shock Cola's

recipe is only known to one other person besides the three that developed it, and those three expended a considerable amount of time and effort in developing the recipe. The manager of Shock Cola took reasonable measures under the circumstances to protect the recipe by keeping the only copy in his desk drawer and not divulging the recipe to anyone else. In addition, Shock Cola's recipe was the sole reason for the company's profitability, and that profitability was in the amount of twenty million dollars a year. Also, a competitor would have had to expend two years of research to duplicate the recipe. Therefore, the court will likely find that Shock Cola satisfies all six elements of the Restatement. Additionally, because the Restatement's six part test is a narrower guideline than MUTSA, and MUTSA is based on the Restatement, the court will likely find that Shock Cola's recipe is a trade secret under the guidelines of MUTSA.

Sample Memo 1

This is an example of a memo from an associate to a client corporation. Note the formal language and structure the associate has used, and how the style differs from the writing sample written in law school. A mid-level to senior associate might send this out without having anyone else review it, but a junior associate would show it to a partner or senior associate before sending it to a client.

LAWYERS ARE US

100 MAIN STREET

Anytown, Anystate xxyxy

TO: Company A

FROM: Associate

RE: Formation of an Internal Revenue Code ("IRC") §501(c)(3) affiliate

In accordance with your request, this memorandum discusses several of the issues related to the formation of tax-exempt organizations under Section 501(c)(3) of the Internal Revenue Code, generally known as charitable organizations.

FACTS:

Company A, is exploring the creation of a nonprofit organization: The Company A Institute for Health (the "Institute"). Like Company A, the Institute will provide medical screening to individuals, but for little or no charge. Additionally, the Institute will perform studies on dietary supplements and their impact on human health in general.

DISCUSSION:

A nonprofit organization is one that is exempt, i.e., excused from paying, federal income tax. While there are a number of methods to qualify as tax exempt, those organizations which are exempt by reason of IRC §501(c)(3) (the "Statute") are generally also charitable donees, i.e., eligible to attract charitable contributions that are deductible to the donor for federal income tax purposes. Accordingly, the organizations that qualify under IRC §501(c)(3) are often referred to as charitable organizations and must meet several qualification criteria discussed below.

Purpose of Organization. Organizations specifically identified as charitable in the Statute are those created and operated exclusively for, among other things, "religious, charitable, scientific, testing for public safety, literary, or educational purposes." Although the tax regulations defining the types of charitable entities do not contain any specific reference to the promotion of health as a charitable purpose, the courts and the IRS have reaffirmed this aspect of charitable activity on several occasions. In addition to public hospitals and HMOs, the various types of health provider institutions which have qualified as charitable organizations include: preferred provider organizations, drug rescue centers, blood banks, halfway houses, and medical research organizations. Additional research in this area will assist us in determining how the provision of medical screening of the appropriate charitable class (discussed below) may qualify the Institute as a charitable purpose under the Statute.

Moreover, contingent upon how the Institute's research data is developed, compiled and disseminated, the study of dietary supplements and their impact on human health may additionally qualify the tax-exempt status of the organization under the category of educational or scientific purposes, or both. The advancement of education includes, among other activities, the advancement of knowledge through research, and dissemination of knowledge by publications, seminars, and lectures. The advancement of science includes comparable activities devoted to the furtherance or promotion of science and the dissemination of scientific knowledge.

Requirement of Charitable Class. The people who are to benefit from the charitable activity must constitute a sufficiently large or indefinite class, e.g., inhabitants of a particular town, employees of a particular company, the elderly, the poor, the distressed, or the handicapped. Organizations which benefit relatives of the donors, or organizations such as social clubs or fraternal organizations generally do not meet the charitable class test. Moreover, a charitable purpose cannot be served where the property involved or the income therefrom is directed to a private use. Thus, a charitable organization cannot be organized and operated for a profit or for other private ends. Subsequent to Company A's identification of the class or classes of individuals to be served by the Institute, we will be able to better evaluate the potential for qualification under the Statute.

Organizational Considerations.

A. Form. The tax-exempt organization must be a legal entity separate and apart from all other entities, and may take one of three (3) forms: a corporation, a trust, or an unincorporated association. It may be either the parent or a subsidiary of or under common control with, another legal entity, irrespective of whether the organizations are tax-exempt or taxable. One entity may control the other either through interlocking directorates, a membership or stock.

B. Governance. Both tax-exempt and for-profit organizations must have a governing board comprised of one or more managers. In a corporation, such mangers are known as directors. In Anystate, a not-for-profit corporation is required to have three (3) directors. An individual may be a member of the Board of more than one organization, including both tax-exempt and for profit organizations. Whether the same individuals sit on the Boards of both the tax-exempt and the for-profit organization is a matter of choice, however, the organizations must remain separate legal entities with their own governing boards, officers, bank accounts, and the like.

Exemption Process:

In order for an organization to qualify as a charitable organization, it must file an application for recognition of the exemption with the IRS and receive a favorable determination letter or a ruling from the IRS to that effect. To receive tax exempt status of and the deductibility of contributions to an organization from the date of its formation, compliance with certain IRS notice rules is necessary. The general rule is that the notice to the IRS, which includes the completed application, must be submitted within 15 months from the end of the month in which the organization was formed under state law.

Conclusion:

Based on the foregoing, it appears that with the development of a qualifying purpose and the selection of a qualifying charitable class to be served, the Institute may, upon the timely filing of its application to the IRS, qualify as a charitable organization under the Statute, either as the parent of Company A or as one of Company A's subsidiaries.

Sample Memo 2

LAWYERS ARE US

100 MAIN STREET

Anytown, Anystate xxyxy

To: Partner

From: Associate

Re: Documentary stamp tax on stock certificates issued out-of-state and later brought back into Anystate

ISSUE

Whether a stock certificate issued outside the Anystate and later brought back into the Anystate triggers the need to pay Anystate documentary stamp taxes on the issued certificate.

BRIEF ANSWER

It depends. Whether documentary stamp taxes would have to be paid depends on whether acts regarding the issuance of the stock certificate take place out-of-state or inside Anystate. The Anystate Supreme Court and the Anystate Department of Revenue (the "Department") have ruled that if all acts relating to the issuance of stock certificates are conducted out-of-state, then stock certificates can be brought back into Anystate without having to pay documentary stamp taxes. However, when acts relating to the issuance of stock certificates take place both inside and outside of Anystate, the answer is not so clear cut. In such instances, the Department balances the various in-state and out-of-state contacts to determine whether there is a nexus between Anystate and the issuance of stock certificates. If the issuance has enough contact with Anystate, then documentary stamp taxes may be imposed.

DISCUSSION

Anystate Statutes

In general, Section 201.01, Anystate Statutes, provides that documents subject to documentary stamp tax are those which are "written or printed by any person who makes, signs, executes, issues, sells, removes, consigns, signs, records or ships the same, or for whose benefit are used, the same are made, signed, executed, issued, sold, removed, consigned, assigned, recorded or shipped into the state." More specifically, Section 201.05(1), Anystate

Statutes, authorizes a tax on "each original issue, whether organization or reorganization, of certificates of stock or shares, however designated, issued in the state."

What is relevant for our purposes is whether the stock certificate is being issued inside or outside of Anystate? In other words, did the stock certificate have enough contact with Anystate to trigger the need to pay Anystate documentary stamp taxes? The Anystate Technical Assistance Advisements issued by the Department have clearly indicated that Section 201.05(1) controls over Section 201.01 when determining whether a stock certificate is issued in the state. See Technical Assistance Advisement No. 95(B)4-005, 1995 Fla. Tax. LEXIS 120 (March 2, 1995).

The Anystate Supreme Court

The Anystate Supreme Court has only once addressed the issue of imposing documentary stamp taxes on issued stock certificates. The Court held that without a definite connection between the issuance of stock certificates and the State of Anystate, documentary stamp tax would not be due. In Anystate Power & Light Co. v. Ray E. Green, 166 So. 2d 146, 147 (1964), the Board of Directors of Anystate Power & Light Company met in the State of New York and authorized the issuance of 400,000 additional shares of common stock, including 1,000 shares of stock issued and delivered in New York. All of the proceedings in connection with the creation, execution, signing, issuance and registration of the 1,000 shares of stock took place in New York. See id. The stock certificates were issued in New York and were not made, assigned, executed, issued, sold, removed, consigned or shipped in Anystate. See id. The New York transfer agent delivered the shares in New York to the stock owners listed in the Company's stock records. See id. Subsequently, copies of the stock lists were taken from the stock records maintained in New York and mailed to the Company's Anystate office. See id.

The issue in Anystate Power & Light Co. was whether the transfer of stock shares would trigger the need to pay documentary stamp taxes. The Court ruled that the transfer was not taxable in Anystate because "there is no definite link, connection or nexus between the State of Anystate and the transfer of the stock certificates." Id. at 148. The Court concluded that "the statutory requirement that copies of stock lists be maintained in the office of the Anystate Power and Light Company in Anystate would not have a material bearing upon the issuance of the stock certificates, nor was such step necessary in the valid issuance of said certificates." Id. Thus, since the stock certificates were issued in New York and all acts predicated to the issuance took place in New York, no tax was due on the stock certificates. Unfortunately, the Court has not addressed instances where the issuance of stock certificates involves contacts both inside and outside of Anystate.

Department of Revenue: Technical Assistance Advisement

The Department has issued opinions on documentary stamp tax matters with fact patterns not so clear cut as Anystate Power & Light Co. In each of the four Technical Assistance Advisements issued by the Department on documentary stamp tax in connection with the issuance of stock certificates, it determined that, without providing much legal analysis, no documentary stamp tax was due on the stock issued.

In Technical Assistance Advisement No. 95(B)4-005 issued March 2, 1995, the Department ruled that no documentary stamp tax was due on a stock issue occurring out-of-state through an out-of-state transfer agent, where the issue was authorized in Anystate by the Company's officers and directors. In this case, the Parent, a Delaware corporation, owned the Company, an Anystate corporation. The Company is a wholly-owned subsidiary of the Parent. The Parent organized a new Anystate Holding Company ("Holding Company") as a wholly-owned subsidiary. After organizing the Holding Company, the Parent transferred all of the stock of the Company to the Holding Company and then distributed on a one-for-one basis stock of the Holding Company to the Parent's stockholders.

The stock transfer agent for both the Parent and the Holding Company was an out-of-state bank. Thus, physical issuance and handling of the stock of the Holding Company was out-of-state, notwithstanding the fact that authorization for such issuance was from the Board of Directors of the Holding Company in Anystate. The Department held that since the original certificates were issued outside of Anystate, documentary stamp tax was not due on the issued certificates. The Department, in reaching its conclusion, relied on the fact that the secretary of the Company carried out all the authorized duties in another state and executed in that state a notarized certificate that the original and subsequent issuances of stock by the transfer agent took place in a state other than Anystate.

Similarly, the Department decided that stock in a Anystate company issued in New York by the Company's transfer agent pursuant to an Automatic Dividend Reinvestment Stock Purchase Plan ("Plan") was not issued in Anystate and thus, not subject to documentary stamp tax. In Technical Assistance Advisement No. 90(B)-4-006, the Company's Board of Directors authorized the creation of a Plan in Anystate. Members of the Plan authorized the Company, as their agent, to secure additional stock of the Company through original issuance under the terms of the Plan into the name of the Company acting as agent and custodian under the Plan documents.

The transfer agent responsible for issuing stock in the Company was located in New York. The Company, as agent for the respective Plan participants, directed the transfer agent in New York by written correspondence to issue a specified number of previously authorized yet unissued shares of common stock in the Company into the Plan name. All cash received for the stock was retained by the Company in Anystate. Subsequently, the transfer agent issued the stock certificates in New York and notified the Company of the issuance of the stock certificates. The stock certificates were then delivered by the transfer agent to an agent of the Company in New York. The agent of the Company made actual delivery of the stock certificates to the Plan offices in Anystate at a subsequent date. The Department determined that even though the Board of Directors authorized the creation of the Plan in Anystate, documentary stamp tax did not apply because the stock certificates were issued in New York. The Department stressed that all acts relating to the issuance were conducted outside of Anystate.

In Technical Assistance Advisement No. 92(B)-4-008, the same Company as in Technical Assistance Advisement No. 90(B)-4-006 modified the way in which it accomplished the same transaction as discussed above. In this case, the Company, as agent for the respective Plan participants, directed the transfer agent in New York by written correspondence to issue a specified number of previously authorized yet unissued shares of common stock in the Company into the Plan's name, pursuant to a book memo account established by the Plan to replace the holding of actual physical certificates by the Plan in Anystate. When individual participants were to receive their certificates, the Company directed the transfer agent in New York to re-register the original issued shares that were outstanding within the book memo account into the name of the individual participant. The certificates were then mailed to Anystate. The re-registered and reissued shares at that point were provided by the Company to the Plan participant.

Here, the Department noted that the issuance of stock mailed into Anystate was a reissued share and thus, no original issue of shares occurred in Anystate. The Department held that "All the acts predicate to the original issuance have occurred in New York and the shares that are held by the plan in the plan's name for the benefit of the participants are issued and outstanding shares for Company's purpose." As such, there was no need to pay documentary tax stamps on the issued stock certificates.

Lastly, the Department concluded that the issuance of new stock on the transfers involved in the reorganization of a large corporation into several regional holding companies was except from documentary stamp tax where the transfer agent performing the issuance function was not present in Anystate, and except for the actual delivery of the stock certificates, all transactions relevant to the reorganization took place outside of Anystate. In Technical Assistance Advisement No. 83(B)-4-024, the Company reorganized into several regional holding companies and issued stock in connection with the reorganization. The Company, a Delaware corporation, had its principle office and facilities in Jacksonville, Anystate. Yet, the Company did not want any of its holding companies to be incorporated in Anystate, own assets in Anystate, nor transact business in Anystate. The Company's transfer agent was registered with the United States Securities and Exchange Commission. The Department determined that except for the delivery of the new certificates to Anystate residents, all transactions incident to this reorganization took place outside of Anystate. Consequently, the Department held that no documentary stamp tax was due on the issuance of stock certificates pursuant to the reorganization.

In conclusion, the Technical Assistance Advisement opinions provide some insight into the various factors the Department weighs when deciding the relationship between the issuance of stock certificates and the contact with Anystate. In each of these four opinions, all transactions relating to the issuance were conducted out-of-state. Unfortunately, the Department has yet to discuss a situation where a company issuing stock certificates engages in certain activities in connection with the issuance both inside and outside Anystate. In such a case, the Department's Technical Assistance Advisement opinions should provide more insight in determining whether the issuance of stock certificates occurs inside or outside of Anystate.

CONCLUSION

Section 201.05(1), Anystate Statutes, the Anystate Supreme Court, and recent Anystate Technical Assistance Advisements issued by the Department indicate that as long as a stock certificate is issued outside of Anystate, then such a certificate may later be brought into Anystate without being subject to Anystate's documentary stamp tax. However, the more contacts with Anystate, the more likely the Department would impose a documentary stamp tax on the issuance of stock certificates.

Sample Memo 3

LAWYERS ARE US

100 MAIN STREET

Anytown, Anystate xxyxy

To: Senior Counsel

From: Associate

Re: Original Document Retention

ISSUE

Whether original documents containing signatures must be retained after being converted by electronic imaging, specifically in the states of Georgia and Florida.

SHORT ANSWER

The main risks in destroying original documents are that retention of the original will be specifically required by law or that the reproduction of the original will not be admissible in a dispute relevant to such document. Our research indicates only one statute in Florida or Georgia, not relevant here, that requires the retention of original documents. With respect to admissibility of reproductions, two statutes have been enacted that address this issue. In addition, Commentators have indicated that microfilm and other duplication methods are regularly admitted as evidence. However, the relevant statutes contain ambiguities that have not yet been clarified by case law. Although we believe that the storage of documents by electronic means would satisfy the requirements of these acts, the safer course of action is to retain the originals.

ANALYSIS

I. GEORGIA

The Uniform Photographic Copies of Business and Public Records as Evidence Act

The Uniform Photographic Copies of Business and Public Records as Evidence Act ("UPA") has been adopted in 33 states and one territory, including Georgia but not Florida, and reflects the mainstream of thinking within the United States relating to the legality of duplicate copies. It has been codified by the Federal government and applies to matters in Federal Court and to governmental entities. See 28 USC §1732 (2000). This Act reads in pertinent part as follows:

"If any business, institution, member of a profession, or any department or agency of government, in the regular course of business or activity has kept or recorded any memorandum, writing, entry, print, representation or combination thereof, of any act, transaction, occurrence, or event, and in the regular course of business has caused any or all of the same to be recorded, copied, or reproduced by any photographic, photostatic, microfilm, microcard, miniature photographic, or other process which accurately reproduces or forms a durable medium for so reproducing the original, the original may be destroyed in the regular course of business unless its preservation is required by law. Such reproduction, when satisfactorily identified, is as admissible in evidence as the original itself in any judicial or administrative proceeding whether the original is in existence or not."

See Id.

As stated above, the original document must be reproduced and destroyed in the ordinary course of business for the reproduction to be admissible as the original itself. Furthermore, if a statute specifically requires the original records to be retained, a duplicate will not suffice. There are few statutes that require the original records to be retained. Georgia has only one such statute, which is not relevant here. The statute requires a bank to keep original records of accounts that have been active for a period of less than twelve months. See O.C.G.A. §7-1-63 (2000). Therefore, a bank may not provide duplicates in lieu of original bank account documents for a new account. Despite the lack of current statutory requirements for the retention of original documents, reliance on the UPA would require constant monitoring of new developments.

The UPA is applicable if the duplication process accurately reproduces the original or forms a durable medium for reproducing the original. There is some question as to whether electronic imaging systems produce accurate reproductions of the original. Electronic images are comprised of small dots. Most scanners have a maximum scanning resolution, which limits the image. The image is reproduced, but the exact number of dots comprising the image of the original will not be apparent in the duplicate. Accordingly, the reproduction is not an exact duplicate of the original. However, this is also the case with microfilm and other duplication methods that are widely accepted into evidence. Electronic imaging systems raise additional issues in that the image is not stored as it is scanned. After scanning, the image is compressed ten or more times by the technique "run length encoding." This technically results in an alteration of the original image. Accordingly, electronic imaging may not be viewed as an accurate reproduction of the original. Therefore, to be an acceptable reproduction under the UPA, the electronic method of reproduction must be deemed a durable medium. There is no available case law defining a durable medium. Consequently, the safer course of action is do retain the original documents until such medium has also become recognized by the courts.

II. FLORIDA

The Uniform Rules of Evidence

The Uniform Rules of Evidence have been adopted by the federal government and at least 28 states and territories, including Florida but not Georgia. This law contains two applicable provisions. Article X Rule 1001 reads in pertinent part as follows:

"An original of a writing or recording is the writing or recording itself or any count intended to have the same effect by a person executing or issuing it. If data is stored in the computer or similar device, any print output readable by sight, shown to reflect the data accurately, is an original."

See Uniform Rules of Evidence § 1001 (2000).

Under this definition, a print output of stored computer data may be considered an original writing for purposes of legal evidence.

However, Article X Rule 1003 limits the general application of this Act to those duplicates as to which authenticity of the original is not questioned. In addition, the Act would not be applied in circumstances in which it would be unfair to admit the duplicate as an original. See Uniform Rules of Evidence § 1003 (2000). There is no pertinent authority defining unfair circumstances. Based on these ambiguities, the original documents should be retained in Florida as well.

CONCLUSION

Although Florida has adopted the Uniform Rules of Evidence and Georgia has adopted the UPA, there are sufficient ambiguities in these statutes to warrant continuing the practice of retaining original documents.

Sample Memo 4

LAWYERS ARE US

100 MAIN STREET

Anytown, Anystate xxyxy

To: Client

From: Lawyers Are Us

Re: Fiduciary Rights and Duties of Corporate Directors and Officers in Anystate

This memorandum discusses in general terms the rights and powers of directors and officers managing a corporation in Anystate. Further, the following summarizes the fiduciary duties of directors and officers to the corporation and its stockholders. Both directors and officers are agents of the corporation and thus, have certain responsibilities to act in good faith and in the corporation's best interest.

The members of a corporation's board of directors exercise the powers of the corporation and manage its direction, subject to restrictions in the corporation's articles of incorporation. In Anystate, each corporation is required to have a board of directors consisting of one or more individuals. The general duties of the board of directors, include, but are not limited to, (1) establishing general corporate policy, including type of business activity, products, pricing, and services; (2) selecting, supervising, and removing officers; (3) initiating corporate transactions, such as mergers, sale of assets or voluntary dissolution. The board of directors may create committees to delegate certain corporate responsibilities, except as otherwise provided in the articles of incorporation or bylaws.

A director may be removed, with or without cause, by the shareholders, unless the articles of incorporation provide that directors may be removed only for cause. If a director is elected by a voting group of shareholders, only the shareholders of that voting group may participate in the vote to remove the director. However, a director may only be removed at a shareholder's meeting if notice of the meeting stated that a purpose of the meeting was removal of the director.

Under Anystate law, a corporation is not required to have any particular officers. Rather, a corporation has the officers described in its bylaws or appointed by the board of directors in accordance with the bylaws. Each officer has the authority and duties as set forth in the bylaws, or to the extent consistent with the bylaws, the duties prescribed by the board of directors. The bylaws or board of directors, however, must delegate to one officer the responsibility for preparing minutes of the directors' and shareholders' meetings and for authenticating records of the corporation. The board of directors may remove any officer at any time with or without cause. Yet, an officer's removal does not otherwise affect the officer's contract rights, if any, with the corporation.

Directors and officers are agents of the corporation. As such, directors and officers have a fiduciary relationship to the corporation and its stockholders. Specifically, both directors and officers owe the corporation and its stockholders a duty of care and duty of loyalty. For those who are both corporate directors and officers, there is an even greater fiduciary duty.

Anystate law requires that a director exercise his or her duties of care (a) in good faith; (b) with the care an ordinary prudent person in a like position would exercise under similar circumstances; and (c) in a manner he reasonably believes to be in the best interest of the corporation. A director who complies with each of these requirements is insulated from liability under the so-called "business judgment rule." Although the Anystate statutes do not define the standard of conduct for officers, officers must generally follow the same principles of acting in good faith and in the corporation's best interest.

If a director, after reasonable investigation and in the absence of a conflict of interest, approves a course of action that he or she honestly and reasonably believes will benefit the corporation, then the business judgment rule insulates the director from liability. Thus, even if a director makes a mistake, he or she is not held liable so long as the decision was made honestly and reasonably. For the business judgment rule to apply, the following elements must be present: (1) the decision under review must be a business decision; (2) the director may not stand to benefit personally from the transaction, such as a self-dealing transaction; and (3) the director must have exercised due care in reaching an informed decision.

In addition to their duty of care, directors and officers have a duty of loyalty to the corporation and its stockholders. For example, a director or officer may not usurp a corporate opportunity. If a director or officer learns of developing business opportunity in which the corporation has an interest, that corporate opportunity must first go the corporation. If a director usurps the opportunity, Anystate imposes a constructive trust in favor of the corporation. Yet, if, after full disclosure of all material facts, the corporation rejects the opportunity, then the director or officer is free to pursue the opportunity.

Further, the duty of loyalty may prevent conflict of interest transactions between the corporation and one or more directors. An example would include a corporation and corporate director being on opposite sides of the same transaction. Such a transaction will not be voided if: (1) disclosure to the board of directors or board committee that authorizes, approves, or ratifies the transaction without counting the votes of interested directors; (2) disclosure of all of the shareholders entitled to vote and that they authorize, approve, or ratify the transaction; or (3) that the transaction was fair and reasonable to the corporation at the time it was authorized. Simply stated, the director must disclose his interest to the disinterested directors or the transaction must be fair to the corporation. Yet, under Anystate case law, corporate officers or directors are not precluded from entering into and engaging in another business enterprise similar to but separate from the corporation if they act in good faith and refrain from interference with the business of the corporation.

In summary, directors and officers must act in good faith and with due care and loyalty to the corporation. As agents, directors and officers must place the goals of the corporation and its stockholders ahead of any personal objectives. In fairness to the corporation, directors and officers must disclose all relevant information to the corporation and its shareholders before using such information for personal gains. Officers and Directors who fail to fulfil their legal duties of care and loyalty subject themselves to liability for damages to the corporation.

Sample Memo 5

LAWYERS ARE US

100 MAIN STREET

Anytown, Anystate xxyxy

To: Partner

From: Associate

Re: Texas Law Re Resolution of Claims Against a Dissolved Corporation

Once a corporation has filed articles of dissolution in Texas, the corporation will continue in existence for a period of three years for the purpose of prosecuting and defending any remaining actions and holding title and liquidating its properties and assets. Tex. Bus. Corp. Act art. 7.12(A) (2001).

Once articles of dissolution have been filed, the corporation will not be liable for any claims, other than claims that existed as of the time of the dissolution. Id. art. 7.12(C). An existing claim is (i) a right of payment, damages, or property, whether liquidated or unliquidated, accrued or contingent, matured or unmatured, that existed before the dissolution and is not otherwise barred by limitations and (ii) a contractual obligation incurred after dissolution. Id. art. 7.12(F). Any claim that existed as of the time of dissolution will be extinguished unless an action or proceeding is brought within three years following the date of dissolution. Id. art. 7.12(C).

A corporation may expedite the three year time period for settling claims by giving written notice to those having or asserting any existing claims against the corporation. Id. art. 7.12(D). This notice must detail when a claim must be presented (which may not be less than 120 days after the date of the notice) and that a failure to make a claim within the required time period will result in extinguishment of the claim. Id. The notice must be accompanied by a copy of the applicable provisions of the Texas Business Corporation Act relating to the extinguishment of claims in dissolution. Id. If the claimant does nothing, the claim will be extinguished. If a claim is made in response to the notice, the corporation may object to it by providing written notice of the objection to the claimant. Id. Following the notice of the objection, the disputed claim will be extinguished unless an action is brought by the claimant against the corporation within 180 days after the notice of rejection or before the expiration of the three year period following the date of dissolution. Id.

Accordingly, if the corporation does not attempt to expedite the settling of claims by employing the afore-mentioned notice, a claimant has the full three year period to bring forward any claim. Moreover, any unknown claimants also would have the full three-year period to make a claim.

Sample Document 1: Service Contract (excerpt)

A corporation uses a service contract for arrangements with consultants or vendors of service. Such a contract might be standardized for all service providers of a different type or tailored to each new business relationship.

SERVICE CONTRACT

This Service Contract (hereinafter "Contract"), dated and effective , 2002, is between ("Contractor"), a (name state here) corporation with offices located at 301 Main Street, Suite 000, Anytown, Anystate 00000 and ("COMPANY"), a (name state here) corporation whose principal offices are located at One Drawbridge Circle, Anytown, Anystate 00000 .

WITNESSETH:

WHEREAS, COMPANY wishes to purchase certain services from Contractor; and

WHEREAS, Contractor is willing to provide such services to COMPANY.

NOW, THEREFORE, for and in consideration of good and valuable consideration, the receipt and sufficiency of which are hereby acknowledged, the parties hereto agree as follows:

1. Term. The term of this Contract is for a period of ( ) months beginning _______________ and ending _______________.

2. Services. The work, hereinafter "Services" to be performed by the Contractor under this Contract are as follows:

(______________________)

Contractor agrees

A. To perform the Services described above at the Rates listed in Exhibit A Attached hereto and made a part hereof. Contractor warrants that the Services shall be performed at a standard at or higher than the industry standard for similar services.

B. To submit monthly invoices with any reports as further described herein to: _________________________

____

____

C. To perform all Services in accordance with applicable law, and to furnish at its expense, all relevant expertise and all items necessary for the performance of the Services.

D. To submit the following reports to COMPANY at no charge in a complete and timely manner:

COMPANY reserves the right to modify or substitute the required Reports during the term of this Contract.

E. To comply in all respects with the applicable laws, codes, rules, regulations and decisions of any legislative, administrative or judicial body exercising any power or jurisdiction over any Services described in this Contract including, but not limited to:

(1) Social Security Laws,
(3) Workers Compensation Laws,
(4) The Occupational Safety and Health Act of 1970, and
(5) All applicable federal, state or local laws regarding drug and/or alcohol testing.

3. Volume. Contractor understands that COMPANY does not guarantee the volume of Services that COMPANY may purchase from Contractor.

4. Non-Disclosure. All information, including but not limited to, financial statements, product information, manufacturing capabilities, passwords, documents, data and business records, that is disclosed to Contractor or that Contractor observes or comes into contact with during the term of this Contract or the rendition of any Services to COMPANY, whether generated by COMPANY or a customer or contractor of COMPANY, shall be deemed "Confidential Information" and the sole and exclusive property of COMPANY. Contractor shall take all reasonable measures to maintain the confidentiality of said Confidential Information by its employees, agents, representatives and couriers. Contractor shall not use the Confidential Information for any purposes other than to perform its obligations hereunder and shall not disclose any Confidential Information to any third party without the prior, written consent of COMPANY. Contractor acknowledges that all right, title, and interest in and to said Confidential Information, including the right to produce, extract, or exhibit to any third party and any intellectual property rights, exist in COMPANY only. Contractor shall return such Confidential Information promptly upon the expiration or termination of this Contract.

It is understood that the confidentiality provisions contained herein shall not apply to any information Contractor can demonstrate by written evidence:

(a) was at the time of disclosure by COMPANY, or thereafter (but prior to disclosure by Contractor) becomes, through no act or failure to act on the part of Contractor, part of the public domain; or

(b) was at the time of disclosure by COMPANY in Contractor's possession and was not acquired directly or indirectly from COMPANY.

Contractor expressly agrees that COMPANY shall be entitled to injunctive and/or other equitable relief in any court of competent jurisdiction to prevent or otherwise restrain a breach of this section of this Contract, provided that the foregoing shall not preclude COMPANY from seeking any and all damages suffered as a result of any unauthorized disclosure by Contractor.

5. Default.

A. If COMPANY makes a determination that Contractor is not in compliance with the provisions of this Contract, it shall notify Contractor in writing and specify such deficiencies. If Contractor has not corrected such deficiencies to COMPANY's reasonable satisfaction within thirty (30) days of the date of COMPANY's notice, COMPANY may immediately cancel the Contract. Upon termination of this Contract in accordance with this subparagraph 5A, COMPANY shall be entitled to: (i) a full refund for all Services for which COMPANY has paid but which Contractor failed to perform or performed incorrectly; (ii) reimbursement for all damages caused by Contractor's default including, but not limited to, any costs incurred by COMPANY in acquiring replacement Services if the cost of the replacement Services is in excess of what COMPANY would have paid Contractor for those Services in accordance with this Contract and (iii) any and all other remedies to which COMPANY is entitled in law or equity.

B. If Contractor makes a determination that COMPANY is not in compliance with the provisions of this Contract, it shall notify COMPANY in writing and specify such deficiencies. If COMPANY has not corrected such deficiencies within thirty (30) days of the date of Contractor's notice, Contractor may cancel the Contract on thirty (30) days' notice. Contractor's sole remedy upon termination in accordance with this subparagraph 5B shall be payment for any Services actually rendered by Contractor through the date of termination.

C. COMPANY may terminate this Contract on 30-day written notice to Contractor without penalty and for any or no reason, including, without limitation, diminished demand for the services, capital constraints and/or Contractor's inability to maintain competitive pricing, quality or quantity of services.

D. If, during the Term of this Contract, the ownership of Contractor changes or if Contractor is purchased or merges with another company, COMPANY shall have the right to immediately terminate this Contract.

E. Upon termination by COMPANY, Contractor shall immediately discontinue all work, thereafter doing only such work as may be necessary to preserve and protect work already in progress.

F. Termination hereunder shall discharge all executory obligations of the parties but shall not affect any right based on a prior breach of performance of this Contract nor affect any right or obligation which is intended to survive such termination.

6. Invoices. All invoices submitted by Contractor must be separated by labor and material charges and, if applicable, by location.

7. Indemnification. Contractor covenants and agrees to indemnify, protect and save harmless COMPANY, including its parent, affiliate and subsidiary companies, and the employees of COMPANY and the aforementioned companies, from and against any and all damages, claims, demands, causes of action, suits, judgments and expenses whatsoever, suffered or incurred by COMPANY, on account of injury to or death of any persons whomsoever (including employees of Contractor and employees of COMPANY or others), or loss or destruction of or damage to property of any kind or character whatsoever, and to whomsoever belonging, hereinafter collectively referred to as "incidents", caused or contributed to by any act or omission, negligent or otherwise, of Contractor, or of any of Contractor's agents, servants or employees, arising out of or incidental to the performance of the Services, except to the extent that the foregoing incidents occurred as a result of the negligence or intentional acts of COMPANY where such negligence or intentional act is the sole proximate cause of the incident(s) for which Contractor seeks to avoid indemnification.

Sample Document 2: Promissory Note

A promissory note is a legally binding contract in which a corporation or an individual promises to repay a certain amount of money. Most promissory notes say, in effect, "I promise to pay you $_____, plus interest of ___ percent," and then describe how and when payments will be made. This is a very basic note. In a corporate law situation, a lawyer would usually draft a related loan agreement.

PROMISSORY NOTE

US $_______________ [date]

_______________, ________[location]

For value received, the undersigned, _________________, an individual residing at ___________________________________ (hereinafter "Maker"), promises to pay to the order of ______________________________, a ___________ corporation whose address is ___________________________________, and its successors or assigns (hereinafter called "________"), the principal sum of _______________ AND NO/100 DOLLARS ($__________), together with interest thereon from the date hereof until the entire principal balance hereof has been paid in full at the rate set forth below and calculated on the basis of a 365-day year, both principal and interest being payable in lawful money of the United States of America, at the address of __________, or at such other place as the holder hereof may designate in writing.

Principal and interest shall be payable in accordance with the following terms, on the following dates, and in the following amounts:

1. **INTEREST RATE:** From the date hereof until the entire principal balance hereof has been paid in full interest shall accrue on the principal balance outstanding from time to time at the rate of ten percent (10%) per annum, compounded annually.

2. **MATURITY:** The entire principal balance plus accrued and unpaid interest thereon shall be due and payable immediately upon written demand of __________, but in any event, no later than 5:00 p.m. Eastern time on ______________, _____. Prior to such time or prior to a demand by __________, Maker shall make payments in accordance with Section 4 below.

3. **PREPAYMENT; APPLICATION OF PAYMENTS:** This Note may be prepaid in full or in part at any time without penalty. All payments shall be applied first to accrued interest, then to principal.

4. **PAYMENTS:** Payments on this Note shall be made as follows: ________________________. Nothing contained in this Section 4 shall prevent __________ from exercising its right to demand payment in full on this Note at any time as provided under Section 2 above.

5. **WAIVERS; CONSENTS:** Maker hereby waives demand, protest and notice of maturity, and all requirements necessary to hold him liable as Maker. Maker consents to any extensions or renewals or modifications of this Note, or any part hereof, without notice, and agrees that he will remain liable as such during any extension or renewal or modification hereof until the debt represented hereby is fully paid.

5. **COSTS OF COLLECTION:** Maker shall pay all costs of collection, including reasonable attorneys' fees, on failure to pay the principal of this Note or any interest thereon at maturity whether suit be brought or not, and whether incurred at trial, on appeal, or in bankruptcy.

6. **INTEREST AFTER DEFAULT:** This Note and all sums due hereunder shall bear interest from the date when due until paid at the lesser of: (i) a rate equal to five (5) percentage points above the then applicable rate set forth in Section 1 above; and (ii) the highest rate permitted by law.

7. **LIMITATION ON INTEREST:** Notwithstanding any provision hereof to the contrary, if any payment deemed to be interest, when added to all other payments deemed to be interest should be in excess of the maximum amount permitted by law to be paid as interest on the actual balance of principal outstanding for the term of the loan, then, in such event, such payment shall be applied to the unpaid principal balance, or, if there be none, shall not be payable, or if paid, shall be refunded.

8. **GOVERNING LAW:** This Note is to be construed according to the laws of __________________.

IN WITNESS WHEREOF, the undersigned has caused this Note to be executed by its duly authorized representative.

____

Sample Document 3: Opinion Letter

An opinion letter is written by a law firm in reference to a merger, acquisition or stock purchase. Corporations require this of the law firms representing them in a transaction as a guarantee that the company they will acquire or merge with has been correctly organized. Each state has different requirements for opinion letters. The following opinion letter is based on the recommendations of the Florida bar association.

Opinion Letter

[date]

Ladies and Gentlemen:

We have acted as special counsel to __________________, a __________ corporation ("__________") in connection with its execution and delivery of that certain Asset Purchase Agreement dated as of ______________ (the "Agreement") by and among __________________________ (collectively, the "Sellers"), __________ and ______________.This opinion is delivered pursuant to Section _________ of the Agreement. Capitalized terms utilized herein that are not otherwise defined herein have the meanings attributed to them in the Agreement.

We have examined a copy of the Agreement and, in addition, we have examined the (a) Articles of Incorporation of __________ and all amendments thereto certified by the Secretary of State of the State of _________, and a true and correct copy of the bylaws of __________, certified by an officer of __________; (b) a certificate of the Secretary of State of the State of __________, certifying as to the active status of __________; and (c) a certificate of the officers of __________ as to, among other things, the incumbency of certain of its officers and certain resolutions of the board of directors with respect to the Agreement, certain other documents required by the Agreement to be executed and delivered by __________ (the "Transaction Documents") and the transactions contemplated by the Agreement and the Transaction Documents (the "Contemplated Transactions"). In addition, we have examined such other instruments, certificates, documents, agreements and written material, and have considered such questions of law (subject to the limitation set forth herein), as we have deemed necessary or appropriate for the purpose of rendering this opinion. As to any facts material to our opinion, we have, when relevant facts were not independently established by us, relied upon the aforesaid instruments, certificates, documents, agreements and written materials. Additionally, when any opinion set forth herein relates to the corporate status or qualification to do business of __________, such opinion is based entirely upon, and is limited by, the certificates of public officials and officers of __________ (as applicable) referred to above.

In performing our examination, we have assumed without inquiry (1) the legal capacity of each natural person; (2) the legal existence of all entities that are parties to the transaction (other than __________); (3) the power and authority of each person or entity (other than __________ or persons acting on behalf of __________) to execute, deliver and perform the Agreement and the Transaction Documents and to do each other act done or to be done by such person or entity, including the taking of all corporate or other action necessary to execute and deliver each such document and to perform all other obligations and otherwise to effect the transactions contemplated thereby; (4) the authorization, execution and delivery by each person or entity (other than __________ or persons acting on behalf of __________) of the Agreement and each Transaction Document to which such person or entity is a party; the legality, validity, binding effect, and enforceability as to each person or entity (other than __________ and persons acting on behalf of __________) of the Agreement and the Transaction Documents and each other act done or to be done by such person or entity in connection therewith; (6) the payment of all required documentary stamps, taxes, and fees imposed upon the execution, filing, transfer, and recording of documents; (7) that there have been no undisclosed modifications of any provision of any document reviewed by us in connection with the rendering of this opinion and no undisclosed prior waiver of any right or any remedy contained in any of the documents; (8) the genuineness of each signature other than that of __________ or persons acting on behalf of __________, the completeness of each document submitted to us, the authenticity of each document reviewed by us as an original, the conformity to an authentic original of each document reviewed by us as a copy; (9) the truth and accuracy of the representations and other statements as to all matters of fact set forth in the Agreement and in the certificates of the officers of __________ and as to all factual matters otherwise not known to us to be untruthful contained in any document encompassed within the due diligence review undertaken by us; (10) the accuracy on the date of this opinion as well as on the date stated in all governmental certifications of each statement as to each factual matter contained in such governmental certifications; (11) that the Sellers have acted in good faith, without notice of adverse claims, and have complied with all laws applicable to them that affect the Agreement and the Contemplated Transactions; (12) that the Contemplated Transactions comply with all tests of good faith, fairness, and conscionability required by law; (13) that routine procedural matters, such as service of process or qualification to do business in the relevant jurisdictions, will be satisfied by the parties seeking to enforce the Agreement; (14) that all statutes, judicial and administrative decisions, rules, and regulations constituting law for which we have assumed responsibility are published in a generally accessible manner; (15) that there are no other agreements or understandings among the parties that would modify the terms of the transaction or the respective rights or obligations of the parties to the Agreement or the Transaction Documents; (16) that there has been no mutual mistake of fact or fraud or duress with respect to the Agreement or the Transaction Documents; (17) the constitutionality and validity of all relevant laws, regulations and agency actions unless a reported case has otherwise held or widespread concern has been expressed by commentators as reflected in materials that lawyers routinely consult; and (18) that the Sellers have obtained all consents required to execute, deliver, and perform their obligations under the Agreement.

We call your attention to the fact that, although we have from time to time acted as counsel to __________, our representation has been limited to individual matters referred to us by the management of __________. Except for examination of the documents enumerated herein, we have made no independent investigation as to the organization, existence or affairs of __________ or the Sellers. Without limiting the generality of the foregoing, we have made no examination of dockets or other public records, except as expressly set forth above.

Any opinions set forth herein concerning the validity, binding effect and enforceability of a particular agreement mean that (x) such agreement constitutes an effective contract under applicable law, (y) such agreement is neither invalid in its entirety because of a specific statutory prohibition or public policy nor is it subject in its entirety to a contractual defense, and (z) subject to the last sentence of this paragraph, a remedy is available upon a material default under such agreement. This opinion does not mean that any particular remedy is available upon a material default or that every provision of such agreement will be upheld or enforced in any or each circumstance by a court. The opinions expressed below are further qualified to the extent that the validity, binding effect and enforceability of any provision of the Agreement, or any agreement or document contemplated thereby or executed in connection therewith, or any rights granted pursuant to the Agreement, any agreement or document contemplated thereby or executed in connection therewith, or obligations incurred thereunder, may be subject to and affected by

(a) applicable bankruptcy, receivership, rehabilitation, liquidation, insolvency, reorganization, moratorium, or other laws affecting the rights and remedies of creditors and secured parties generally;

(b) general principals of equity (regardless of whether considered in a proceeding in equity or at law) and the exercise of equitable powers by a court of competent jurisdiction (and no opinion is expressed herein as to any specific or equitable relief of any kind or as to the availability of equitable remedies); and

(c) applicable state and Federal laws relating to fraudulent conveyances and fraudulent transfers and to indemnification for violations of securities laws.

In addition, our opinions should not be construed to provide any opinion regarding the validity, binding effect or enforceability of (I) provisions to the effect that failure to exercise, or delay in exercising, rights or remedies will not operate as a waiver of any such right or remedy or (II) disclaimers, liability limitations with respect to third parties, releases, legal or equitable discharge of defenses, liquidated damages provisions, provisions purporting to waive the benefit of statutory or common law rights, or provisions releasing a party from, or indemnifying a party against, liability for its own wrongful or grossly negligent acts.

Based upon and subject to the foregoing, we are of the opinion that

1. __________ has been incorporated under the _________ Business Corporation Act (or comparable _________ statute in effect at the time of incorporation) and its status is active.

2. __________ has the corporate power to conduct its business and to execute and deliver the Agreement and the Transaction Documents and to perform its obligations under the Agreement and the Transaction Documents.

3. __________ has authorized the execution, delivery and performance of the Agreement and the Transaction Documents by all necessary corporate action.

4. The Agreement and the Transaction Documents have been executed and delivered by __________.

5. Subject to the limitations contained herein, the Agreement and the Transaction Documents are valid and binding obligations of __________ enforceable against __________ under the law of the State of __________ and the Federal law of the United States of America.

We express no opinion herein as to the laws of any jurisdiction other than the law of the State of ______________, and the Federal law of the United States of America and assume no responsibility for the applicability or effect of any other laws. The opinions rendered herein are being delivered solely to you and for your sole benefit in connection with the Agreement and may not be relied upon by you for any other purpose or relied upon by or furnished to any other party or in any other transaction without our prior written consent.

This opinion relates solely to matters existing as of the date hereof and we disclaim any obligation to update this opinion for events occurring after such date.

Very truly yours,

____

Partner, Law Firm of Smith, Jones

Sample Document 4: Limited Liability Company Operating Agreement

Every corporate entity needs an organization document. This is the organizational document for a limited liability company. A limited liability company (LLC) combines attributes from both corporations and partnerships. It gives the entity protection from personal liability for business debts, as would a corporation, and it provides the simpler tax structure of a partnership.

Limited Liability Ccompany

Operating Agreement

This Limited Liability Company Operating Agreement (the "Agreement") is made and entered into as of this ___ day of, by and among

____

____

pursuant to the provisions of the Delaware Limited Liability Company Act, §18-101 et seq. (the "Delaware Act"), in accordance with the provisions set forth below.

WITNESSETH:

WHEREAS, ___________ and _____________ recognize their complementary strengths and expertise in ( );

NOW, THEREFORE, in consideration of the mutual agreements, promises, and undertakings hereinafter set forth, _____________ (collectively, the "Parties") agree as follows:

ARTICLE I.

Definitions

Section 1.01 Definitions; Rules of Construction. Capitalized terms not otherwise defined herein shall have the meanings as set forth on Appendix A attached hereto. Words used herein, regardless of the number and gender used, shall be deemed and construed to include any other number, singular or plural, and any other gender, masculine, feminine, or neuter, as the context requires.

ARTICLE II.

Organization

Section 2.01 Name; Formation. The name of the Company shall be ____________________. The formation of the Company through the execution and filing of the Certificate of Formation of the Company with the Secretary of State of the State of Delaware on July 25, 2001, setting forth the information required by Section 18-201 of the Delaware Act is hereby confirmed, ratified and approved.

Section 2.02 Purpose. The purpose of the Company shall be to engage in any lawful business that may be engaged in by a limited liability company organized under the Delaware Act, as such business activities may be determined by the Members from time to time. Such activities shall include but shall not be limited to the following (and the Company may contract with third parties (or the Members themselves) to perform any of the following activities upon the agreement of the Members):

(a)

Offices. The principal office of the Company, and such additional offices as the Members may establish, shall be located in ________________________, or at such place or places inside or outside the State of Delaware but within the United States as the Members may designate from time to time. The registered office of the Company in the State of Delaware is located at 1111 Company Street, in the City of Wilmington, County of New Castle.

ARTICLE III.

Representations and Warranties

Section 3.01 Representations and Warranties of (_____). (_____) hereby represents and warrants as follows:

(a) (_____) is a corporation duly organized, validly existing and in good standing under the laws of (____). (______) has the corporate power and authority to own, lease, and operate its assets, properties, and businesses and to enter into this Agreement and to carry out its obligations hereunder. The execution, delivery and performance of this Agreement have been duly authorized by all necessary corporate action on the part of (_____), and this Agreement is legally binding upon (_____) in accordance with its terms.

(b) The execution, delivery, and performance by (_____) of this Agreement and the transactions contemplated hereby will not (i) violate the provisions of any order, judgment, or decree of any court or other governmental agency applicable to (_____) or the organizational documents of (_____); (ii) result in a material breach of or constitute a material default under any contract or agreement to which (_____) is a party or by which (_____) is bound; or (iii) violate any provision of law of the United States of America or any state thereof, the violation of which is likely to have a material adverse effect on the business, operations or condition of (_____) or the Company.

Section 3.02 Representations and Warranties of (_____). (_____) hereby represents and warrants as follows:

(a) (_____)is a corporation duly organized, validly existing and in good standing under the laws of the State of (_____). (_____) has the corporate power and authority to own, lease, and operate its assets, properties, and businesses and to enter into this Agreement and to carry out its obligations hereunder. The execution, delivery and performance of this Agreement have been duly authorized by all necessary corporate action on the part of (_____), and this Agreement is legally binding upon (_____) in accordance with its terms.

(b) The execution, delivery, and performance by (_____) of this Agreement and the transactions contemplated hereby will not (i) violate the provisions of any order, judgment, or decree of any court or other governmental agency applicable to ___________ or the organizational documents of (_____); (ii) result in a material breach of or constitute a material default under any contract or agreement to which (_____) is a party or by which (_____) is bound; or (iii) violate any provision of laws of the United States of America or any state thereof or Canada, the violation of which is likely to have a material adverse effect on the business, operations or condition of (_____) or the Company.

ARTICLE IV.

Capital Structure

Section 4.01 Members' Interests and Capital Contributions.

(a) The Interests assigned to (_____) and (_____) are as follows:

Member	Interest
(_____)	%
(_____)	%

(b) (_____) will contribute the following property to the Company on the date hereof or as soon as practicable:

(i) (_____)

(c) (_____) will contribute the following property and cash to the Company on the date hereof or as soon as practicable:

(i) (_____)

ARTICLE V.

Future Financing of the Company/Allocations/Distributions

Section 5.01 Future Financing. The Members anticipate that in the future the Company may require additional funds for working capital requirements or capital expenditures. Any such additional funding shall be obtained from any of the following sources as may be approved by the Members:

(a) cash reserves of the Company;

(b) loans to be obtained from banks and other such independent sources, in which event, the Members shall exert reasonable efforts to assist the Company in obtaining any such loans;

(c) additional capital contributions made to the Company by the Members, in amounts determined by mutual agreement of the Members;

(d) loans to be made to the Company by (i) the Members and/or (ii) a Related Company of either of the Members; or

(e) any other funding source mutually agreed upon by the Members.

Web Sites and Other Resources

Law schools

www.lsac.org
The Law School Admission Council

Law school rankings

www.usnews.com/usnews/edu/grad/rankings/law/lawindex.htm
U.S. News & World Report law school rankings

www.lsac.org/LSAC.asp?url=/lsac/deans-speak-out-rankings.asp
"Law School Deans Speak out Against US News Rankings," an LSAC letter endorsed by the deans of 178 law schools

www.ilrg.com/rankings
"Judging the Law Schools," an alternative ranking of American law schools by a former Chief Justice of the Michigan Supreme Court

monoborg.law.indiana.edu/LawRank/index.html
"The Ranking Game," yet another method of ranking, from the Indiana University School of Law-Bloomington

www.bc.edu/bc_org/svp/carct/matrix.html
The Boston College Law School Locator lists the 25th to 75th percentile LSAT scores and GPA ranges of first-year classes at accredited law schools to help you gauge your chances of admission.

Law firms

www.martindale.com
The Martindale-Hubbell Legal Network, including access to The Martindale-Hubbell Law Directory of law firms and lawyers worldwide.

www.law.vault.com
Vault's portal to the inside scoop on the legal industry. Resources include a job board, free newsletters, the Electronic WaterCooler™ (where associates can vent on firm-specific message boards) and a career library.

Law firm rankings

The Vault Guide to the Top 100 Law Firms
Vault's annual guide to the nation's top law firms is based on surveys of thousands of associates and includes in-depth firm profiles as well as prestige and quality of life rankings.

www.nlj.com/nlj250
The NLJ 250, The National Law Journal's annual survey of the largest law firms in the United States, includes information about firm size, associate salaries and other perks such as moving/bar study expenses and signing bonuses.

www.law.com/special/professionals/amlaw/2002/amlaw100/amlaw_100main.shtml
The Am Law 100, The American Lawyer's list of the nation's top-grossing law firms

Federal government agencies

www.cia.gov
Central Intelligence Agency (CIA)

www.cftc.gov
Commodity Futures Trading Commission (CFTC)

www.fcc.gov
Federal Communications Commission (FCC)

www.fdic.gov
Federal Deposit Insurance Corporation (FDIC)

www.ftc.gov
Federal Trade Commission (FTC)

www.usdoj.gov
United States Department of Justice

www.sec.gov
U.S. Securities and Exchange Commission (SEC)

www.opm.gov
United States Office of Personnel Management (OPM)

Other job search resources

law.vault.com
Vault's Law Career Channel features hundreds of law job listings, law firm profiles, compensation information, a directory of legal recruiters and more.

www.nalp.org
The National Association for Law Placement

www.nalpdirectory.com
The 2003-2004 NALP Directory of Legal Employers

www.pslawnet.org
PSLawNet, The Public Service Law Network Worldwide

www.idealist.org
Idealist's Nonprofit Career Center lists hundreds of nonprofit job and internship opportunities.

www.attorneyjobs.com
Federal Reports Inc.'s Legal Career Center offers subscription access to Attorney Jobs Online.

www.nylawyer.com
New York Lawyer offers a wealth of information for new lawyers, including firm-related news, a law firm recruiting guide, and tracking of associate pay and layoffs.

About the Author

Zahie El Kouri

Zahie El Kouri is a freelance writer and instructor of writing in Jacksonville, Florida. She received her J.D. from Cornell Law School and her M.F.A. in Fiction Writing from New School University. She is a former corporate associate of LeBoeuf, Lamb, Greene & MacRae.